Correctional Psychology

themes and problems in correcting the offender

Correctional Psychology

themes and problems in correcting the offender

Robert J. Wicks

center for correctional training
new york city department of correction

institute of criminal justice
st. john's university

ⵁ canfield press   san francisco
a department of harper & row, publishers, inc.
new york • evanston • london

Correctional Psychology: Themes and Problems
  in Correcting the Offender

Cover photograph and design: judy sidonie tillinger

Library of Congress Cataloging in Publication Data

Wicks, Robert J
   Correctional psychology.

   Bibliography: p.
   1. Correctional psychology. I. Title.
[DNLM: 1. Criminal psychology. 2. Social adjust-
ment. 3. Social service. HV7428 W637c 1974]
HV9275.W43   364.6'01'9   73-22351
ISBN 0-06-389345-2

     75 76 77   10 9 8 7 6 5 4 3

For my daughter, Michaele Aileen

CONTENTS

Contents

Contents

FOREWORD

Chief Justice Warren Burger has cautioned that "Correctional systems that do not correct will merely aggravate the problem of crime and the public safety." To be sure, nothing can be more fundamental to the operation of a successful correctional rehabilitation program than the employment of well trained personnel who are sensitive to the needs of the men and women in their charge. In order to ensure this goal, criminal justice experts have recognized the need for sound, well documented and readable research to serve as the basis for correctional training programs.

Never has the need been more pressing for a comprehensive study in the area of correctional psychology. In the past, numerous articles have explored and analyzed the various aspects of this field, but not until the publication of CORRECTIONAL PSYCHOLOGY: Themes and Problems in Correcting the Offender has there been an attempt to produce a single, basic unifying volume.

This work not only supplies social workers, nurses, correction officers, psychological interns, parole officers and other correctional personnel with sound, practical advice, but also offers the introductory student a fundamental program of instruction. Likewise, this work is of value to the average citizen as well, since everyone has a responsibility, if not an obligation, to be aware of and help improve the correctional system. As members of the society to which the offender must return, each of us must be concerned with his state of mind and the steps that are taken to treat him. CORRECTIONAL PSYCHOLOGY conveys this awareness to its readers.

Robert Wicks has explained himself clearly and consistently. The reader venturing into correctional psychology for the first time may be assured that this book is as accurate as it is readable. The work itself is comprehensive in that it embodies a number of the more timely and extensive studies in the field.

CORRECTIONAL PSYCHOLOGY: Themes and Problems in Correcting the Offender is an ideal supplementary text for almost any criminal justice course (especially penology, criminology, introduction to corrections), a fine source book for professionals in the field, and an excellent introductory volume for the informed adult who wishes to become more aware of the correctional psychology area. In essence, CORRECTIONAL PSYCHOLOGY is a book which has much to offer to those who fortunately choose to read it.

George E. Ansalone, Director
Institute of Criminal Justice
St. Vincent's College
St. John's University

PREFACE

During the past decade, interest in penology has been growing rapidly. This interest has logically spilled over into the allied field of correctional psychology, which in turn has expanded at an impressive pace.

Correctional psychologists and allied behavioral scientists have recently produced a great deal of excellent instructive material. However, students in the field are still having some difficulty forming an overview of new developments since most texts so far have been collections of previously published articles, rather than basic original works.

In light of the increasing number of present and future students of correctional psychology, penology, criminology, and criminal justice, the need for a general basic text is clear. CORRECTIONAL PSYCHOLOGY: Themes and Problems in Correcting the Offender is a product of the desire to fill this void. It is designed to be as comprehensive as possible, in line with the goals of correctional psychology as expressed by the American Association of Correctional Psychologists. These include learning to understand offender behavior, helping offenders to function more effectively on an intellectual, social, and emotional level, and thus assisting offenders in adjusting successfully to society.

In other words, this book is not concerned simply with the role of the correctional psychologist. It will not retrace the steps of existing introductory corrections texts. Instead, CORRECTIONAL PSYCHOLOGY is directly concerned with offender rehabilitation and the total correctional setting, either in the penal institution or in the community. It is designed to provide an overview of the methods and problems involved in treating the offender. In addition, it may also spur greater interest in corrections, one of the most crucial problems facing modern society.

The book opens with a section on classification, which leads into a discussion of different
types of therapy currently in use. Case studies
and reports on each therapy indicate how effective it seems to be in the field. Special problems and new approaches in corrections are then
examined: prison violence and sexuality, conflicts between custodial and treatment staffs,
educational and vocational programs for offenders,
programs involving paraprofessionals, and the
important work being done with community corrections. The last chapter probes the future of
correctional psychology.

An extensive bibliography of books, articles,
and reports dealing with these and other aspects
of correctional psychology can be found at the
back of the book. At the end of each chapter,
there is an annotated list of core references.

This volume should provide the student with
a basic introduction to the most current themes
and problems in correcting the offender. Accordingly, it is designed to serve as a core text in
such courses as: correctional psychology,
institutional treatment of the offender, and
correctional counseling. Furthermore, as a
supplementary text, its objective is to add a
further dimension to courses in criminal justice,
penology, criminology, juvenile procedures,
probation and parole, and correctional administration.

Besides all the dedicated workers in the
fields of psychology, social work, and correc-
tions, there are several groups and individuals
to whom I owe thanks. To the staff of the
Information Center at the National Council on
Crime and Delinquency, I wish to express my deep-
est appreciation. To Annette Sputo, who typed
this manuscript, I also extend my thanks.
George E. Ansalone of St. Vincent's College, St.
John's University, Stanley L. Brodsky of the
University of Alabama, Patrick M. Flanagan of
Long Beach City College, G. M. Gilbert of Long
Island University, Robert B. Mills, University of

Cincinnati, David Schmidt, Chief Psychologist at
San Quentin, and John L. Sullivan of Pasadena City
College gave advice and criticism where they were
most needed. And to my wife Michaele, for her
constant encouragement and support, there are no
words that can say how grateful I am to this
beautiful woman.

R.J.W.

INTRODUCTION

Psychology has as much of a place in the correctional setting as it does in the free community. As a helping profession, it can assist the offender whether he is incarcerated in a maximum security prison or on probation with only minimum supervision. Thus, correctional psychology is flexible and can operate in many areas. Generally, though, the behavioral or social scientist in the penal setting is concerned with one or more of five main areas: classification, treatment, training, research, and evaluation.

Classification is a means of providing information about each prisoner to those who must make decisions that affect him. Using the classification methods discussed in Chapter 1, the psychologist can help the custodial staff determine how to best house, care for, and rehabilitate him. This not only makes more appropriate treatment possible, but also simplifies the basic problems of institutional security.

Psychological treatment for the offender theoretically can range from psychoanalysis to a behavioristic approach. Different treatments can be conducted by a professional or by a trained, supervised paraprofessional. Therapy may be carried out on a one-to-one basis, or in a group setting.

Training, like offender treatment, can take many forms according to the psychologist's goals and techniques. He may instruct with audio-visual aids, through a formal lecture, or by encouraging fellow staff members to share their impressions in a group setting.

Research, as well as training, can deal with almost any area related to the welfare of the offender. Particular areas that concern the psychologist and his fellow staff members (social workers, psychiatrists, mental health workers)

Introduction

include causes and prevention of institutional
riots, suicidal behavior, prison sexuality,
offender programs, and the feasibility of community-based corrections (halfway houses, probation,
group homes).

Because critical evaluation of almost any
serious proposal may come under the direction of
a correctional psychologist, he can spend much of
his time in program evaluation. This may take in
projects as different as a suicide prevention
program and an inmate plan to redecorate the
cafeteria.

Within this general framework, numerous
techniques and issues have emerged in the field
of correctional psychology. From the theories,
examples, and studies we will discuss, the
current and predicted trends in correctional
psychology should become clear.

CHAPTER 1

Prisoner
Classification

Tests, questionnaires, and other devices used by
psychologists have been under continual fire for
their inaccuracies in portraying man's vital
nature. Yet, despite the arguments and prejudices
against such devices, behavioral scientists continue to measure human reactions and capacities.

Because of their practical value, classification methods have spilled over from the community
at large to the penal setting. Some large institutions have refined and expanded measuring techniques considerably. Furthermore, a growing number
of small facilities as well have added evaluation
techniques to their correction programs.

CLASSIFICATION AND THE PSYCHOLOGIST

To conduct these programs, however, the local
correctional administrator needs assistance. The
town jailer of TV Westerns, who usually knew his
charges and had time to give them personal attention, is a rarity now. With prisons constantly
overflowing with new criminals, it is a feat for
the chief jailer to remember his confinees' names,
much less be aware of their individual problems
and needs. But even with the added difficulties
of administering a large modern penal institution,

1

the warden has more responsibility now than ever before for the welfare of the inmates assigned to his facility. With the advice and help of his directors of security and treatment, he is able, and expected, to make significant decisions on how each prisoner is housed and treated.

The most efficient way to collect and organize the data needed for these decisions is to use classification tools. First, of course, these tools must be developed and administered by someone trained in measuring inmates' intellectual and personality status. The person best equipped for this task is the correctional psychologist.

CLASSIFICATION AS A MANAGEMENT TOOL

Probably the most obvious aim of a correction facility is security. The community should be safe from the dangerous offender. The weak inmate must be protected from aggressive prisoners. These goals must be accomplished at the lowest possible cost. Segregation cells and close surveillance equipment are, clearly, an expensive way to solve the problem. An effective classification system, then, not only can help set up and maintain good security, but also can save money.

One of the main decisions regarding security, made soon after an offender enters the reception area of a prison, concerns housing. Some considerations, of course, are evident; for example, male and female prisoners are put in different quarters. But classification can uncover other considerations as well: Weak, passive prisoners must be separated from those who are aggressive and domineering; prisoners with severe physical handicaps should be housed on the main floor; and young first-time offenders should not be held with older, seasoned prisoners.[1]

[1]Mark S. Richmond, Classification of Jail Prisoners, U.S. Bureau of Prisons, Washington, 1971, p. 1.

Another important reason for immediate classification is to prevent undue health problems. In addition to special housing for the handicapped, prison officials need to arrange prompt medical or psychological attention for the physically ill or behaviorally bizarre person.

Procedural problems, too, must be noted promptly. Since an inmate's physical health is tied closely to his mental health and the other goals of correctional treatment, the psychologist must ensure that his assistants screening incoming prisoners pick up minor as well as major health needs, such as those involving special diets.

Another area where classification can provide guidelines is prisoner work assignments. Security is one factor the correctional psychologist must consider here. He also needs to know the policies of the institution he is dealing with regarding questions such as work assignments in general, work release candidates, and selecting trustees. Beyond that, classification should pinpoint any mental or physical problems that would affect a prisoner's ability to do the work required, as well as any aptitude, skills, or experience that would suit him for a particular job.[2]

As far as the warden is concerned, then, classification processes should provide him with information that will help him identify each prisoner's status in order to make management decisions. This identification indicates how the inmate stands legally, mentally, physically, and emotionally. In other words, the chief jailer should be able to answer questions about each confinee such as: Is he sentenced? Does he have a high school diploma? Is he suffering from any physical disease? What, if any, are his major psychological problems?

[2]Ibid., p. 2.

Prisoner Classification

On the basis of this information, the correctional administrator can make informed decisions on prisoner assignments as well as educated predictions of inmates' behavior while incarcerated. Through classification and reclassification, each inmate can be placed in the situations and among the people most conducive to good management. Not only is this essential to keep the prison running smoothly, but as one study indicated, it also improves the odds that the therapeutic programs will be successful.[3]

Classification can also act as a check on whether administrative decisions and policy are producing the desired results. By comparing classification data to statistics on the reactions of the inmates to certain types of housing, programs, and occupations, management procedures can be kept vital. In the past, penal institutions often have been choked by their own adherence to unworkable, tradition-bound policies and regulations. Classification can help prison officials to make informed decisions, and can help those directing security and treatment programs to continually re-examine the broad principles underlying those procedural decisions.

CLASSIFICATION AS AN AID TO EFFECTIVE TREATMENT

For a long time, the only goal in penology seemed to be keeping prisoners submissive. If an inmate was not passive enough and did not conform readily (wasn't "prison" or "con" wise), the official assumed he simply needed to be pressured. Various techniques were used to force the prisoner, who was believed to have a basic common criminal personality, to submit and become obedient. Today, most penologists and correctional psychologists reject the idea of a

[3]U.S. Prisons Bureau, Project R.E.A.D.Y. (Reaching Effectively Acting-out Delinquent Youths), U.S. Government Printing Office, 1968.

4

"criminal personality" and realize that any kind
of treatment will have different impacts on different types of offenders.[4]

Although at least five treatment approaches
in recent years have consistently produced positive results (see Chapters 2-4), it seems fairly
certain that none of them is equally effective
with all types of offenders. The psychologist
must match the type of treatment with the offender
if recidivism (repetition of an offense) is to be
lowered. Here again, classification of inmates
can be useful.

Differential Treatment

Offenders differ in many ways besides the
form of their offenses. The reason someone
breaks the law, for example, varies according to
the type of problem he has. The impetus to commit a crime may result from any number of over-
lapping causes, including family problems, poor
self-control, poverty, an identity crisis, or
membership in a deviant subculture.[5]

The theory of differential treatment grew
out of two studies whose findings indicated that
the impact of both individual and group therapies
would vary according to the type of offender with
which they were used. Since this was the case, a
therapy that worked with one offender might have
no results, or negative results, with another.
Thus, any benefit an approach might have could
easily be masked, or even canceled out, if some
of the inmates to whom it was applied were not

[4]Frank Gibson and Raymond Payne, "Personality and
classification in criminal corrections," American Journal
of Correction, 30(3):7-8, 10, 27, 1968.

[5]Marguerite Q. Warren, "The case of differential
treatment of delinquents," Canadian Journal of Corrections,
October, 1970, 12, No. 4.

receptive to it because of their personality type.[6]

Since the publication of these two studies, a number of subsequent ones have supported their findings. In one report from California, and a similar one from Denmark, individual counseling was found effective with cases of mid-range difficulty, while having little benefit with those classed as easier or more difficult.[7] Another study, done at the Medical Facility in the California Department of Correction, indicated that although group therapy seemed effective with robbers and check forgers, it had a negative impact on offenders involved in crimes against persons. Group therapy, in their case, evidently decreased their ability to adjust to the community.[8] The list of program evaluations that have demonstrated the need for differential therapeutic approaches goes on and on.[9]

[6]J. D. Grant and M. Q. Grant, "A group dynamics approach to the treatment of nonconformists in the Navy," The Annals of the American Academy of Political and Social Science, 1959, 322, 126-135. Also, S. A. Adams, "Interaction between individual interview therapy and treatment amenability in older youth authority wards," California State Board of Corrections Monograph, 1961, 2, 27-44.

[7]J. Havel, "Special interview parole unit, phase IV; a high base expectancy study," California Department of Corrections, Research Report No. 10, June 1963. Also, K. Berntsen and K. O. Christiansen, "A resocialization experiment with short-term offenders," in Scandinavian Studies of Criminology, Tavistock, London, 1965.

[8]T. L. Clanon and C. Jew, "Follow-up of the effects of psychotherapy of prisoners," California Department of Corrections, Vacaville (mimeo), 1969.

[9]For a more complete list see Classification for Treatment, prepared by Marguerite Q. Warren, Center for Training in Differential Treatment, Sacramento, California.

Implementing Differential Treatment

Several years ago, investigators in the field recognized that many institutional programs were failing because they lacked distinct treatment goals and seemed to find multifaceted programs too complex to set up. To deal with these problems, the researchers created a specific strategy called the Preston Typology. The Preston study favored the following:

1. Organizing wards according to offender and treatment types.
   2. Matching staff to the wards according to their particular therapeutic philosophies and interests.
3. Training staff members in principles of classification and familiarizing them with the treatment approaches decided upon by the staff directors.
4. Developing of differential treatment strategies for each class of offender in the institution.[10]

I-level

To organize wards according to treatment-related types, the Preston researchers used the Interpersonal Maturity Classification System (I-level). The California Youth Department also now employs the I-level system. This system is a re-evaluated expansion of the Sullivan, Grant and Grant formulation of the Levels of Interpersonal Maturity, which proposes that personality integration follows a certain sequence in normal childhood development.[11]

[10] Carl F. Jesness, "Differential treatment of delinquents in institutions," in National Association of Training Schools and Juvenile Agencies, Proceedings: 63rd annual meeting, June 1967, Anaheim, California, edited by Jack C. Pulliam, pp. 141-144.

[11] California Youth Authority, "What Is I-level?" California Youth Authority Quarterly, 22(3):3-6, 1969.

Prisoner Classification

The I-level, devised by Warren and Grahm, sets up seven levels of interpersonal maturity. These levels range from the least mature to an ideal of social maturity. Everyone does not move all the way through the scale. Most people proceed beyond level one, the level at which we are born, but stop at an intermediate level rather than achieving the ideal stage seven.

Delinquents generally fall in levels two through five, though rarely level five. In expanding and refining the scale, Warren eventually broke down levels two through four into the following nine subtypes: asocial, aggressive; asocial, passive; conformist, immature; conformist, cultural; manipulator; neurotic, acting-out; neurotic, anxious; situational emotional reaction; and cultural identifier.

Psychologists at the Community Treatment Project in California, who are the leading advocates of I-level, believe that offenders should be classified according to these nine subtypes, so that each inmate can be matched with the best environment, therapy, and work assignment for his personality. Differential treatment strategies, in other words, should be tailored to each subgroup.

DIFFERENTIAL TREATMENT IN ACTION

The Robert F. Kennedy Youth Center, in Morgantown, West Virginia, also uses differential treatment. However, the Center applies it somewhat differently from the Community Treatment Project and the many other California institutions that have adopted it. The Center uses a classification method developed by Dr. Hubert C. Quay, which divides delinquent behavior into four types: inadequate-immature, neurotic-conflicted, unsocialized-aggressive or psychopathic, and socialized or subcultural. (These characteristics also appear in emotionally disturbed and normal persons. The "normal" person either

8

exhibits the tendencies less, or controls them better.)

Within each of these four categories, offenders are classified further by means of three instruments set up by Dr. Quay: a checklist of behavioral problems, completed by correctional officers and counselors who have observed the boy; a true-false questionnaire, filled out by the boy himself; and a checklist on his life history, based on his presentence report. Other measuring devices and techniques not only match the subject to the most effective therapy, but also match staff to the cottage programs where they can be most productive.[12] An individual program, written in terms the youth can understand, is also set up for each offender. The Center's overall program provides for as many different therapeutic approaches as are needed for the varied types of juveniles to be treated.[13]

CLASSIFICATION METHODS

Differential treatment centers generally use one or more of four techniques to classify inmates and ultimately match them to types of therapy. These methods are the self-report form, situational testing, interviews, and observing the inmate while he works.[14]

The self-report, in which the offender is asked to comment honestly on himself, is easy to administer and can provide a wealth of material

[12] Roy Gerard, "Institutional innovations in juvenile corrections," Federal Probation, December, 1970.

[13] Roy Gerard et al., "Differential treatment: a way to begin," Robert F. Kennedy Youth Center, Morgantown, West Virginia (mimeo), May, 1969.

[14] Ted Palmer, "An overview of matching in the Community Treatment Project." Presented at the annual meeting of the Western Psychological Association, San Diego, California (mimeo), March, 1968.

for classification and counseling. In spite of the inmate's natural biases, and the possibility he may try to change the results of the self-report by lying, the information gathered can still be of great help when considered along with the data obtained from other tests and reports.

Objective and projective tests have been used in the correctional setting for a long time. A projective test is one where the subject is given unstructured material (an ink blot, for example) and asked for his interpretation of it. This method is designed to tap the individual's "unconscious mind" and provide some insight into his underlying mental make-up. An objective test poses questions or problems for the subject to answer or solve. It can be a simple sentence completion or a test as detailed and extensive as the 566-item Minnesota Multiphasic Personality Inventory (MMPI), which was originally designed as an aid in psychiatric diagnosis. One way the MMPI has been applied in corrections is as a predictor of change with habitual sex offenders, and further evaluation will probably reveal many other ways it can be valuable.[15] The Sixteen Personality Factor Questionnaire (16 PF) has worked well as a large-scale screening instrument, and the California Psychological Inventory seems to be effective as a supplementary technique with selected cases. The list of tests being tried out in the penal setting is growing longer and longer.

Although tests are constantly becoming more accurate and more applicable to corrections, psychologists still rely heavily on the interview. The informal or formal interview is at the heart of the classification process for differential treatment. It is also the essential element in practically every facility's process of evaluation to see how each inmate is progressing.

[15] Washington State, Western State Hospital, "Effect of treatment as measured by the Minnesota Multiphasic Personality Inventory," Fort Steilacoom, Washington (mimeo), 1971.

Classification certainly has proved a boon to correctional rehabilitation and a fine aid in determining how inmates should be managed and housed. However, several problems still face the psychologist who employs these evaluative tools. The primary objection to classification is that it often stigmatizes its subjects, since many of the terms commonly used to describe deviant behavior have negative connotations. Psychologists and staff must also guard against the problem of the self-fulfilling prophecy. "Labeling" an offender may encourage him to carry out the role in which he has been cast.[16] In addition, anyone who is labeled for any reason often appears to live up to his classification, whether his pattern of behavior really fits it or just has some elements of the category.

The other general objection to classification is that the systems used in most facilities are inadequate. For example, a woman, who has committed a violent crime of passion may have done it on impulse. Yet, because of the nature of her crime, she would be housed and managed in some institutions as though she were someone prone to violent outbursts.[17] Most critics of classification do not seem to want it eliminated, but they do want it further refined so that the methods of grouping inmates are more specific.

Classification systems today are geared to the realization that there is no common criminal personality, and no single cure for crime. With the help of evaluation tools, offenders can now be grouped according to personality type and

[16] Marvin Wolfgang, "The specific viable future: how do we get there?" in University of Alberta, "The prevention of crime in medium-sized cities: some innovations in correctional practice," 1968.

[17] Anthony Roskowski, Rita Silverman, and Helen Hinkel, "Actuarial assessment of criminality in women," Criminology, 9(2/3):166-184, 1971.

11

matched with the most appropriate therapeutic approaches. In accomplishing this, correctional treatment may have moved closer to solving the problem of recidivism than ever before—an ironic but gratifying outcome for a movement whose original impetus was the need for security.

CORE REFERENCES

Classification

Warren, Marguerite. Classification of Offenders as an Aid to Efficient Management and Effective Treatment. Prepared for the President's Commission of Law Enforcement and Administration of Justice, Task Force on Corrections. Washington, D.C., 1966.
A thorough introduction to classification.

Differential Treatment

Warren, Marguerite. "The case for differential treatment of delinquents," Canadian Journal of Corrections, October, 1970, 12, No. 4.
A discussion of the need for and values of differential treatment.

CHAPTER 2

Reality Therapy and Transactional Analysis

Marketing fur parkas in the equatorial city of
Entebbe would undoubtedly be futile. No matter
how enterprising a clothing jobber might be, if he
didn't take climatic conditions into account he
would be doomed to failure. In selling coats, as
in almost any pursuit involving human beings, the
practitioner must suit his approach to his target
population as well as to his own theories if it is
to be effective.

Psychologists' recognition of this simple
principle is evidenced by the variety of therapeutic approaches now in use. Although all these
approaches have achieved at least limited success
with at least one form of behavioral problem, most
techniques have had more impact on one type of
personality disorder than on others. For example,
the behavioristic method now appears to be more
effective with sociopaths than is lengthy,
in-depth psychoanalysis.

Since correctional psychologists come from a
variety of backgrounds and have dealt with nearly
every conceivable psychological problem, we can
assume that every widely accepted therapeutic
philosophy has probably been tried out in a penal
setting at some time. We will limit our discussion to those major techniques that seem to be

most successful in correctional institutions today. (This excludes behaviorism, which will receive separate treatment in Chapter 4.) These methods are reality therapy, transactional analysis, the therapeutic community, and guided group interaction. Of the four, one technique in particular has received increasing attention in the western part of the United States and in Great Britain. It is referred to as reality therapy.

REALITY THERAPY

Freud could not be ignored in his time. His revolutionary theories and striking personality wouldn't allow it. Today theorists are still reacting to his work, and going beyond it with their own.

> Theories of personality are multiplying like the plague. The diseases can take the form of types or traits, factors or fields, canalizations or cathexes. Unlike most epidemics, however, this one is allowed to rage unchecked. It almost seems to be more fun for the doctor to get the bug himself than to try to discover what caused the victim to die. The prognosis in such cases must be deemed, in the vernacular, guarded.[1]

Two of the practitioners who have found Freudian psychoanalytic procedures ineffective and who can be included among those who have contracted "the bug" are Los Angeles psychiatrists William Glasser and G. L. Harrington. Together they have contributed significantly to the development of reality therapy. Unlike many other bugs, though, this one may have curative effects, especially in the correctional field.

[1]Gerald S. Blum, Psychoanalytic Theories of Personality, McGraw-Hill, New York, 1953, p. vii.

14

The success claimed by the Ventura School for
Girls of the California Youth Authority, where
reality therapy is applied, offers support for a
positive appraisal of it.

Mentally Ill?

In reality therapy, the therapist becomes
personally involved with the patient in an effort
to get him to face life and accept responsibility.
According to proponents of reality therapy, people
who have serious problems dealing with life, such
as those classed as neurotic or psychotic, are not
mentally ill in the conventional sense of the
term. Instead, such persons lack a sense of
responsibility and are unable to fulfill their
basic needs. The type and severity of their problems depend upon how they are dealing with
reality. If therapy is to succeed, it must teach
these people to fulfill their needs within the
confines of reality. In other words, reality
therapy is founded on the theory that every human
being has social needs that must be met, such as
the need to love and be loved and the need to feel
that he is unique and important. When a person is
unable to meet these needs through normal social
contacts, he often resorts to unrealistic, and
sometimes antisocial, means to fulfill them.

Reality Therapy versus
Conventional Psychiatry

To understand why Dr. Glasser says reality
therapy differs from the conventional "camp," one
must be familiar with how he sees conventional
therapy. In summary, Dr. Glasser believes "conventional therapists" hold the following tenets:

1. Mentally ill individuals exist, and should
be categorized and treated accordingly.
2. The psychological roots (in the past) of
a problem must be known if treatment is to be
effective.
3. Transference and insight are necessary.
(Transference refers to the situation in which a

patient transfers attitudes he has, or had, toward
people in his past life to the therapist.)
    4. The patient must become aware of his
unconscious forces.
    5. Morality is an issue to be avoided.
    6. The patient must understand what his prob-
lems are and how they affect him before he can
adopt proper behavior patterns—not vice versa.
    7. The therapist should be impersonal and
objective and avoid becoming involved with the
patient.[2]

Glasser defines the differences between
conventional and reality therapy, then, as
follows:

> 1. Because we do not accept the concept of
> mental illness, the patient cannot become
> involved with us as a mentally ill person
> who has no responsibility for his behavior.
>
> 2. Working in the present and toward the
> future, we do not get involved with the
> patient's history because we can neither
> change what happened to him nor accept the
> fact that he is limited by his past.
>
> 3. We relate to patients as ourselves, not
> as transference figures.
>
> 4. We do not look for unconscious conflicts
> or the reasons for them. A patient cannot
> become involved with us by excusing his
> behavior on the basis of unconscious
> motivations.
>
> 5. We emphasize the morality of behavior.
> We face the issue of right and wrong which
> we believe solidifies the involvement, in
> contrast to conventional psychiatrists who
> do not make the distinction between right
> and wrong, feeling it would be detrimental

[2]William Glasser, Reality Therapy, Harper & Row,
New York, 1965, pp. 42-44.

to attaining the transference relationship
they seek.

6. We teach patients better ways to fulfill
their needs. The proper involvement will
not be maintained unless the patient is
helped to find more satisfactory patterns
of behavior. Conventional therapists do
not feel that teaching better behavior is
part of therapy.[3]

Application

Reality therapy is designed to be a learning
experience for the patient. It involves three
steps. First, the patient must form an honest
personal relationship with his therapist. This
can be extremely difficult, especially with a
young, sensitive first offender. (By virtue of
his needing assistance, the patient is assumed
to have had difficulties with interpersonal relationships in the past.) Next, the therapist must
indicate to the patient that he understands, but
does not condone, his irresponsible behavior.
The patient's behavior is rejected, but he himself is accepted. Finally, the therapist teaches
the patient better ways to fulfill his needs
within the framework of reality (society as it
exists).

Reality therapy deals directly with the
patient's conscious, immediate situation.
Accordingly, the therapist begins by outlining
for the patient some tentative goals for treatment, and explaining how reality therapy works.
Timing is of the essence in this approach. The
psychiatrist must see the patient when he is
ready for treatment; a patient who is put on a
waiting list may be in trouble again by the time
he is eventually treated.[4]

[3]Excerpts from pp. 44-45 in Reality Therapy by William
Glasser, M.D. Copyright © 1965 by William Glasser, M.D.
Reprinted by permission of Harper & Row, Publishers, Inc.

[4]Benjamin I. Coleman, "Reality therapy with
offenders: practice," and Melitta Schmideberg, "Reality

17

Reality Therapy, Transactional Analysis

A reality therapy program was developed at Western State Hospital in Washington to provide the control, re-education, and community reintegration necessary for the rehabilitation of sexual offenders. The subjects for this study were picked on the basis of their motivation to change. Treatment included vigorous self-examination, intensive involvement with others, and constant demands for honest and responsible behavior. Small patient groups chose their own leaders and were held accountable for their own custody and treatment. The staff's role was to establish standards and expectations, teach, guide, and provide supplementary administrative and clinical services. When an offender showed responsible behavior in his relationships with other offenders and his family, and during psychotherapy, work and recreational activities, he was recommended for conditional release. Although the study has not been followed up in depth, hospital records indicate only an 8.9 percent re-arrest rate from 1958 to 1968, which suggests that the program was successful.[5]

Case Study

In the study done at Western State Hospital, one of the conclusions psychiatrists reached was that the reality therapy approach would probably be useful with alcoholics and drug addicts. The following case illustrates how reality therapy worked with one young, embittered offender who had been involved with drugs.

John was a black, unemployed 17-year-old, convicted of armed robbery in New York, where he had lived for most of his life. Records of his

therapy with offenders: principle," International Journal of Offender Therapy, 1970, 14(1).

[5]George J. MacDonald, Robinson Williams, and H. R. Nichols, "Treatment of the sex offender," Western State Hospital, Fort Steilacoom, Washington, 1968.

background showed that he came from an inadequate
home—his mother was often absent, his father was
an alcoholic. John left school to work for a
trucking firm when he was 16. Before his convic-
tion, he had previously been arrested three times
for possession of marijuana and "works" (hypo-
dermic needle and other drug paraphernalia).

When John first entered therapy, he spent a
good deal of time detailing his disadvantaged
background and berating the society around him for
the way it had perpetuated his poverty and continued to reject him. He also verbally attacked the
therapist for being part of the system. He condemned the therapist as rich, condescending,
unfeeling, and prejudiced to try to force him to
become angry and reject him as others had done in
the past.

In response to John's attempts to stir him
to anger, the psychologist showed no negative
emotion. Instead, he allowed the confinee to
release his feelings of hostility freely. When
John calmed down, the therapist discussed with
him the tentative goals they had mentioned during
the initial session.

After seven sessions, John started to show
some trust for the psychologist and began to
believe in him as a person, not just as a professional assigned to help him. However, many years
of being rejected by family and friends had made
him quite wary of becoming attached to anyone for
fear of being hurt and abandoned. Consequently,
during the eighth session he tested the therapist
again by telling him he didn't want to come any
more. He claimed he preferred to stay in the
cell-block.

John clearly expected the therapist to react
to this announcement emotionally, since he had
spent considerable time with him and seemed to
have achieved some success. It thus came as a
surprise to John when the therapist simply replied
to the challenge with a question: "How will stay-
ing in the block and leaving therapy help you?"

After being confronted this way with the real consequences of his request to end therapy, John tried once more to see if he could put off the psychologist by telling him unpleasant, degrading things he had done in the past. John related in vivid terms some of the things he had done to get money for drugs. The following is one such story:

> Once I went into a small candy store and asked for something I knew the owner would have to go into the back room to get. While the owner was out of the store, I reached over and took the money from the Heart Association canister standing next to the cash register. A college student walking into the store caught me, but I got away by grabbing a compass and stabbing him in the hand when he tried to stop me.

When he finished telling this melodramatic story, John looked for at least a nonverbal expression of disgust on the face of the therapist. He was caught off guard, though, for the psychologist did not grimace, but said in a frank manner, "Now that you've told me these things, am I supposed to think ill of you?" And he smiled.

After this episode John seemed to realize that he could really count on the therapist. The first phase of therapy had substantially been completed; the relationship between John and the therapist was cemented.

As therapy continued, the psychologist drew John's attention to the unsuccessful results of his irresponsible behavior. Slowly, but steadily, they worked together to formulate a concrete, detailed plan for the future. They also discussed the excuses he had used for failure in the past and how they would threaten him in the future since he could employ them easily as a "cop-out."

A year after he was released from prison, John sent a letter to the psychologist (a rare

20

occurrence in itself), saying,

> . . . I'm not working two jobs anymore. I got promoted in one and the money I make is enough to pay the rent on my apartment in the Village. Man, is it ever good to be out of [there].

> . . . I start school in the Fall. The forms are filled out and the fee paid—you see I take care of all the details now, so I won't back out.

> . . . Everything's not rosey, but I got a couple of girls and . . . I know it's going to get better.[6]

Impact of Reality Therapy

Reality therapy, then, seems to be an effective way of treating some types of offenders. It has other advantages as well: For example, it offers paraprofessionals a wider role in the therapeutic setting. Since the theory behind reality therapy is not as complex as in conventional psychoanalysis, trained paraprofessionals can easily learn to help treat patients. And as other personnel besides clinical psychologists and psychiatrists take part in therapy, more patients can be treated. Another consequence of using reality therapy might be better continuity between prison treatment and parole supervision. Both the reality therapist and the parole officer believe that the criminal must be held responsible for the consequences of his behavior, and that he must learn to see his behavior in terms of right and wrong. An offender who has accepted these

---

[6]"John" was a patient treated by the author. For another case study that illustrates in detail how reality therapy can be used, see the Appendix.

21

Reality Therapy, Transactional Analysis

concepts in therapy within the institution might well adjust more easily to parole and the street environment.[7]

Criticisms of Reality Therapy

Although reality therapy shows strong promise as a method of treating offenders, it has been criticized as well as praised. One reviewer of Glasser's book, Reality Therapy, felt that the stress on the therapist's values might encourage authoritarian and paternalistic attitudes in therapeutic practice.[8] Primarily, despite claims by Glasser that it is unique, reality therapy still has much in common with other therapies currently in use. Accordingly, some observers contend that it is unlikely to be significantly more effective than other similar methods of treatment. Furthermore, although reality therapy is not as complex and time-consuming as psychoanalysis, the psychologist or paraprofessional who uses it will still need extensive training. And even its so-called "short-term" approach may take over a year to be effective with some patients.

However, though some critics warn against or disregard reality therapy as a technique, it is already being used extensively in today's penal settings. Thus, it is essential for those interested and involved in the fields of correctional psychology and penology to be familiar with this form of treatment.

[7]John R. Ackerman, "Reality therapy approach to probation and parole supervision," Probation and Parole, 1969, 1(1), pp. 15-17.

[8]Rodney G. Loper, "Essay review: Glasser's reality therapy," National Catholic Guidance Conference Journal, 1968, 12(4), pp. 287-288.

TRANSACTIONAL ANALYSIS

Transactional analysts believe they are closer to the secret of human behavior than ever before. Games People Play and I'm OK—You're OK, recent popular books based on the principles of transactional analysis, have become overwhelming best sellers. And over a thousand psychiatrists, psychologists, social workers, and professionals have already been trained in this new therapeutic approach.[9] Obviously, transactional analysis— also known as TA—has attracted quite a bit of attention in a short time.

Assumptions of TA

A transaction, in the sense TA uses the word, is a unit of social intercourse; for example, a conversation. The first object of TA is to teach the patient to be aware of the different kinds of social interaction he uses to deal with others. Several special techniques help accomplish this broad goal. One of TA's outstanding features is its vocabulary, which consists of only five words: Parent, Adult, Child, Game, and Script. According to Dr. Eric Berne, who founded the approach, TA's simple terminology and operational nature make it unusually easy to understand and apply.[10]

Another of TA's basic tenets comes from a study by Wilder Penfield. This study indicated that the human memory acts as a three-track tape. During (roughly) the first five years of life it records (1) events the subject experiences, (2) the meaning he attaches to them, and (3) the emotions he feels as they happen. Each person

[9]Richard C. Nicholson, "Transactional Analysis: a new method for helping the offender," Federal Probation, Vol. XXXIV, No. 3, September, 1970, p. 29.

[10]Eric Berne, Principles of Group Treatment, Oxford University Press, New York, 1966, p. 214.

23

often plays back his tape as he faces similar situations later in his life.[11]

Parent, Adult, and Child

Berne also postulated that three maturity levels exist in all people throughout their lives: Parent, Adult, and Child (PAC). These, he feels,"are not concepts like Superego, Ego and Id . . . but phenomenological realities."[12] Berne's belief that these three states exist resulted from his observations of his patients.

> While watching and listening to his patients, Berne noticed that they would change right before his eyes. He observed changes in facial expressions, postures, gestures, voice intonations, vocabulary, and body functions (blushing, etc.). A father's face will harden when his son defies him; a person turns pale and trembles when stopped by the red light and siren of a pursuing traffic officer; an adult person shouts with child-like excitement when his slot machine hits the jackpot and the winning bell clangs. Such changes can be observed in the same person. . . .

> According to Berne, these changes are shifts from one "ego state" to another, like the previously described patient who would feel like a small child at one time, and like an adult at another time. The shifts occur between our Parent, Adult and Child (PAC).[13]

The Parent in everyone is a mental recording of his experiences with figures of authority

[11] Wilder Penfield, "Memory mechanisms," Archives of Neurology and Psychiatry, 67, 1952, pp. 178-179.

[12] Eric Berne, Transactional Analysis in Psychotherapy, Grove Press, New York, 1961, p. 24.

[13] Nicholson, op. cit., p. 30.

during the first five years of his life. This
tape, like the Adult and Child tapes, significantly influences one's life. Each person continually has two "ego states" to contend with:
One corresponds to the current external and
psychological situation, while the other is a
playback of occurrences from early childhood.
The Parent is the sum of all the rules that were
set down for the subject as a young child by his
parent figures (which today could even be the
staff of a popular television show). A person in
the Parent state may be condescending and author-
itative.

Like the Parent, the Child is a state to
which someone can shift at practically any time.
In contrast to the Parent tape of external
events, the Child recording, which was made
simultaneously with the Parent in the subject's
early childhood, is internal. It is a collection
of his positive and negative reactions to the
events recorded on the Parent tape. The way a
person deals later on with feelings such as
anger, frustration, and abandonment, as well as
creativity and curiosity, is deeply affected by
how and when these emotions originally occurred.
The presence of the Child in each person can be
seen in the way a mature adult sometimes acts
frivolously or lets loose his temper as a small
child might.

The Adult does not come into being at the
same time as the other two states, but begins at
about ten months of age when the child starts to
master his environment. As he grows and matures,
his Adult state operates more extensively and
effectively. The Adult is a reality-oriented
state, capable of rejecting or accepting the
Parent tape. "My mother said, 'Don't run on
cement, because if you fall, you'll hurt yourself'; she was right. Dad said, 'Spinach tastes
good'; he was wrong." Similarly, the Adult can
decide when the Child should be let out. During
a board meeting, being silly might not be appropriate, but when relaxing and playing with one's
children it might.

The Adult can also turn off the "not OK" feelings of his Child tape. No matter how benevolent a child's parents might be, he sometimes may feel rejected and depressed because of the reaction he gets when he spills catsup on the floor, for example. If this "not OK" feeling repeats itself in adulthood, as when a person spills his coffee, the Adult state can turn it off instead of letting it upset him. So the Adult is an extremely important state, according to the transactional analyst; as will be seen later, the goal for treatment with TA is to free the Adult so it can deal objectively with the Parent and Child.

Four Life Positions

A life position is a relationship one perceives between himself and others. There are four possible life positions, according to TA: I'M NOT OK—YOU'RE OK, I'M NOT OK—YOU'RE NOT OK, I'M OK—YOU'RE NOT OK, and I'M OK—YOU'RE OK. Each person takes one of these emotional positions early in life, and uses it as a backdrop for his interactions throughout his life.

I'M NOT OK—YOU'RE OK is the common, natural position of every little child. Since a child is often corrected by his parents, he often feels he's NOT OK. However, the parents upon whom he must depend give him attention and affection, so they must be OK.

I'M NOT OK—YOU'RE NOT OK is experienced when the child becomes older and is no longer babied as much as he was originally, causing him to have doubts about the OK status of his parents. The exception to this process is when a child experiences this second position before the initial one (I'M NOT OK—YOU'RE OK). This skip occurs when a baby does not receive enough stimulation or fondling. Such a child becomes autistic (excessively preoccupied with fantasy) and may become a schizophrenic adult.

The third life position is I'M OK—YOU'RE
NOT OK. This is the position taken by a brutal-
ized child, who believes that no one is basically
good (OK) and that he can make it only if left to
himself. Sociopaths and those termed "incorri-
gibles" return to this position when dealing with
others.

Unlike the other three life positions, which
operate on the unconscious level and are based on
feelings, the fourth, I'M OK—YOU'RE OK, is objective and must be actively sought. It results
from a desire to change; the goal of TA is to
convince its patients to seek and ultimately
attain this position.

Games and Transactions

I'M NOT OK—YOU'RE OK, the first life position, is the most common one. Many people in this
position try to make it more tolerable by playing
games. In TA, a game is a series of transactions
that moves toward a well-defined, predictable
outcome. Berne describes it as "a series of
moves with a snare or 'gimmick.'"[14] One game he
mentions is "Blemish," where the subject tries to
find something wrong with a new person he has
met in order to feel more secure about his own
position.[15] To move from the I'M NOT OK—YOU'RE
OK position to the fourth one, I'M OK—YOU'RE OK,
a person must realize that he is playing games and
recognize what they are.

To move to the I'M OK—YOU'RE OK position,
an individual must also be aware of the part his
three ego states (PAC) play when he acts and
communicates with others. When a person speaks
in a sarcastic, condescending way to his brother,
his Parent is speaking. When he is exceptionally

[14] Eric Berne, Games People Play, Grove Press, New
York, 1964, p. 48.

[15] Ibid., pp. 111-113.

defensive and emotional, his Child is showing.
Transactional analysis helps the patient learn to
examine his transactions and recognize his ego
states. When he reaches the point where his
Parent, Adult, and Child are clearly separated,
and the Adult is in control and admits the
"examined Parent" and "adapted Child" when appropriate, then his transactions are ideal.

Transactional Analysis with Offenders

Advocates of TA feel this type of therapy
may have much to contribute to offender treatment
on a number of different fronts. For one thing,
TA explores the games both treatment staffs and
offenders play that hinder rehabilitation. Martin
Groder notes in one article that although therapists have been encouraged to recognize and drop
the games they themselves play, they have sometimes replaced a discarded game with another one.
One such game therapists sometimes play is "KIUD"
(Keep It Up Doc). Here the therapist surrounds
himself with patients who can be counted on to
tell him what a good job he is doing, even if his
work is actually ineffectual.[16] This can be
particularly dangerous in the penal setting, as
is another related game, "HDIGO."

HDIGO (How Do I Get Out Of Here) was examined by Paul McCormick in a recent article. In
this game both the staff and the patients try to
look good: the patients so they can be released,
the staff so they can feel they have helped the
patients. In listing some of the rules of the
game, the author hits a sensitive chord with many
professionals in the field today. "Don't look too
good too soon" and "Do some 'acting out' for
about two months" are games prison-wise offenders
play to manipulate the therapy setting.[17] Everyone

[16] Martin G. Groder, "KIUD," Transactional Analysis
Journal, 1:2, April, 1971, p. 19.

[17] Paul McCormick, "Why institutionalized offenders
don't have to get better," Transactional Analysis Bulletin,
Vol. 4, No. 14.

in the correctional psychology field must have
been fooled at some time by an inmate who made
himself look good so he could terminate his treatment early and get out of jail sooner. Proponents
of TA are right to provide such timely warnings
about the problem of games.

Another aid transactional analysts say they
can offer is the ordinary, easy psychological
language they use in the treatment process and
even in psychological reports. However, Lois
Johnson claimed that in her work with delinquents,
even the TA terminology must sometimes be altered
so the patients can understand it. She felt it
was helpful to change the Parent ego state to
"The Man," the Adult to "Cool Head," and the
Child to "The Kid" when explaining TA to delinquents.[18]

Application

TA has recently won considerable attention
and acceptance in corrections and is being tried
out in many facilities. The federal probation
office for the Eastern District of California
is now using TA, as is the Synanon Community
model program in the U.S. Penitentiary in Marion,
Illinois. Under the direction of Martin Groder,
the Synanon inmates learned to recognize and
understand the games they played, the transactions
they were involved in, and, generally, the ways
they had been living. Groder's work with TA
principles in Illinois, and the work done by
others such as Franklin Ernst,[19] have produced
impressive enough results to suggest that TA may
have great potential in modern penology.

[18] Lois M. Johnson, "TA with juvenile delinquents,"
Transactional Analysis Bulletin, Vol. III, No. 30, p. 31.

[19] Franklin H. Ernst and William C. Keating,
"Psychiatric treatment of the California felon," The
American Journal of Psychiatry, April, 1964.

Reality Therapy, Transactional Analysis

Final Comments on Transactional Analysis

At a time when the pessimism of many correctional workers is rising along with the recidivism rate, the enthusiasm of TA's proponents is most welcome. However, like any new approach, TA could easily be overestimated. Once the excitement over its new jargon and different therapeutic emphasis subsides, TA's popularity may pass the way of other techniques that turned out to be fads. TA appears to have helped many people—some of them offenders—to achieve greater independence and personal growth. However, it will take a conclusive study to prove that TA's results are as significant as they seem to be—particularly in the correctional field. Such data should be available soon, since a number of penal settings now employ TA. With this information, correctional psychologists should be able to tell what kind of role transactional analysis can be expected to play in correcting the offender.

CORE REFERENCES

Reality Therapy

Glasser, William. Reality Therapy. New York: Harper & Row, 1965.
A lively and carefully written account of the theory and practice of reality therapy.

International Journal of Offender Therapy, 1970, 14(1).
A collection of well-written articles on the use of reality therapy in the correctional setting.

Transactional Analysis

Harris, Thomas A. I'M OK—YOU'RE OK. New York: Harper & Row, 1959.
A practical guide to transactional analysis.

Berne, Eric. <u>Games People Play</u>. New York:
Grove Press, 1964.
Examples and explanations of the games
people use in their everyday interactions.

Nicholson, Richard C. "Transactional
Analysis: a new method for helping offenders,"
<u>Federal Probation</u>, Vol. XXXIV, No. 3, September,
1970.
An account of how TA has been and can be
applied in corrections.

CHAPTER 3

Therapeutic Community and Guided Group Interaction

Inadequate staffing can greatly limit the potential of any kind of correctional treatment. To be successful, a rehabilitative technique should be resourceful enough to take full advantage of available talent. Two approaches that are being applied now in the correction setting were developed with a realization of the need to make better use of both professional and paraprofessional staff: the therapeutic community and guided group interaction.

THERAPEUTIC COMMUNITY

For a treatment method to be called "innovative" by major theorists and practitioners, it would surely have to be notably different from the main approaches already in use. The therapeutic community (TC) claimed to be an innovative technique by virtue of its emphasis on the social environment within institutions, at a time when the psychoanalytic model still dominated the field.

The TC, like most types of treatment, did not completely reject other therapeutic styles. In fact, any approach, ranging from psychoanalysis and its concern with inner conflicts to

33

behaviorism and its external orientation, can be
included in a therapeutic community. However, the
TC staff usually invests most of its energies in
social activities—group dynamics, continual examination of environments such as family, work, and
hospital, and designing methods to improve communications between staff and patients.

Maxwell Jones

Few movements are the product of one individual. In this respect the therapeutic community is
no exception; its current form evolved from the
contributions of numerous behavioral scientists.
Still, the TC did receive so much of its impetus
from one person that he can be considered its
prime mover. This dedicated worker is the British
psychiatrist, Maxwell Jones.

Jones's ideas grew out of the work of Adolf
Meyer, who advocated a psychobiological approach
to therapy. Psychobiology is a school of thought
that is concerned with the individual as a whole
biological unit. Its advocates see treatment as
a process in which the therapist can diminish his
patient's negative qualities by emphasizing his
assets. To accomplish this, the patient's talents
and problem areas must be identified in a bio-
graphical summary starting with his birth.

Jones came into contact with psychobiology
while working for five years at the University of
Edinburgh, under Sir David Henderson, a professor
of psychiatry whose techniques were based largely
on Meyer's theories. Jones's interest in Meyer's
social methods accelerated in 1941 when he
directed a psychiatric unit providing treatment
for military personnel. During this first experience with therapy in large groups, he became
convinced that "people living together in hospital,
whether patients or staff, derived great benefit
from examining, in daily community meetings, what
they were doing and why they were doing it."[1]

[1] Maxwell Jones, Social Psychiatry in Practice, Penguin
Books, Baltimore, 1968, pp. 16-17.

After World War II, Jones developed his
theories further while treating British prisoners
of war, "misfits," and patients with character
disorders. During this period, which lasted about
12 years, he formulated his ideas into a therapeutic approach. In 1959 and 1960 he finally
introduced the therapeutic community to American
mental health personnel at Stanford University and
Oregon State Hospital. By the end of this two-
year visit to the United States, his theories
about the social organization of hospitals, daily
community meetings, staff sessions, and the therapeutic community in general were being widely
examined. Eventually these concepts would be
applied in treatment centers throughout the
Western world.

TC Organization

The patients in a TC are expected to take an
active part in their own therapy, as well as in
the other patients' treatment process and in the
overall operation of the therapeutic unit. This
kind of involvement is quite different from the
usual passive role assumed by patients in conventional hospitals. In the traditional hospital a
democratic social structure is rare. It is not
easy to break down the authority barrier between
staff and patients. Nurses and doctors are often
just as reluctant to give up their white uniforms
as patients are to drop their cloak of irresponsibility.

Tradition dies slowly or not at all. When a
therapist recommends involving patients in
hospital government, he runs up against defenses
on both sides of the treatment wire that can prevent or retard the process. However, if a
patient government or council gradually can be
formed in spite of resistance, it can aid immeasurably in the development and maintenance of a TC.

The extent of the patient council's authority will vary from one TC to another. The council
may handle practical matters such as completing
duty rosters and regulating patient privileges, as

well as overseeing jobs such as hospital file
clerk or timekeeper that may be filled by
patients.[2] Where the council has the capacity,
it can also share serious responsibilities with
staff, dealing with such problems as strained
staff-patient relations, reclassifying patients,
and handling difficult members of the community.
Involving patients in managing themselves this
way can help the TC personnel to snap them out
of their indifference, improve their self-images,
and teach them to be more self-reliant.

Along with its advantages, though, releasing
authority to patients can cause problems if it is
not carefully regulated. The staff should give
patients only as much responsibility as they can
handle. When a patient council has worked
together effectively for some time, it may carry
a great deal of responsibility. But if several
of the more healthy patients leave within a short
time and are replaced by new patients who do not
function as well, the staff must assume more
authority until they feel the council is once
again ready for it.[3]

In a sense, the TC, in giving the patients
as much authority as they can handle, is antici-
pating the patient's future, when he will be in a
similar but larger environment with no one to make
decisions for him. As in the TC, he will have to
direct his own life, and, to some extent, the
lives of others as well.

Communication

Personality conflicts that constrict the flow
of information between staff and patients, as well
as among members of each group, can prevent treatment in a TC from being effective. To keep

[2]Maxwell Jones, "Towards a clarification of the
therapeutic community," British Journal of Medical Psychology, 1960, 33, p. 67.

[3]Jones, Social Psychiatry in Practice, p. 100.

communication free and open, certain formal and
informal procedures are built into the TC. The
various daily meetings held in the community seem
to be especially helpful in curbing potential friction between TC patients and staff. Probably the
most important of these sessions is the community
meeting, since it provides an opportunity for all
inmates and personnel to meet together, re-examine
the status of the TC, and discuss each other's
roles in keeping it alive.

As one might expect, in the formative stages
of the TC, there is often considerable resistance
to organizing a community. New staff members, or
patients who are coming from a traditional hospital setting and feel threatened by this new
approach, are particularly likely to balk at such
a switch from the standard therapeutic structure.
If handled correctly, though, the community meeting should be able to melt many of the interpersonal barriers put up by those in attendance.

A typical community meeting may include as
many as 100 patients and 20-30 staff. At this
session, all participants are encouraged to
express their feelings on any subject that affects
the community and themselves. They also discuss
recent actions of the patient council. Such feedback from other members of the community should
provide the council with insight and support, and
keep it in touch with the pulse of the population.
Without these meetings, the council could become
as isolated and hence as ineffective as the well-
known "ivory tower" type of administrator. The
council cannot function as it was designed to
without staff supervision and continual exposure
to peer reaction.

Often the attitudes expressed at these large
community meetings become the subject of subsequent smaller sessions of 8-17 members. Thus the
community meeting also provides a chance for staff
to determine who would fit best into each smaller
therapy group.

Therapeutic Community, Guided Group

Staff Review

Although the community meeting helps the staff
to see how the patients perceive them, it is advisable to hold an additional meeting solely for the
staff. Usually this review of staff attitudes and
efforts occurs immediately after the community
meeting and lasts no more than 45 minutes, so that
participants will not tire of constant meetings
and consequently react negatively to them.

At the community meeting patients are encouraged to take part in their own treatment—a role
traditionally reserved for the hospital staff.
During the staff review, the concept of involving
all members of the community in the treatment
process moves a step further. Nurses, social
workers, and other mental health personnel, as
well as the psychologists and psychiatrists are
encouraged to take active roles in treatment, since
they all come into frequent close contact with the
patients. This realignment of rehabilitative
responsibilities is not meant to demean the
psychologist's position, but to make the most
possible use of the other staff members' talents.

These review sessions give staff members an
opportunity to air and resolve personal tensions
and speak freely about whatever problems they feel
the group should consider. As in the community
meeting, this kind of open discussion helps each
member of the group to feel secure about his own
position and confident about the goals of the
community, and encourages him to be flexible and
creative in his work.

In the same vein, decisions at the staff
review result from a consensus rather than the
decree of a single administrative official.
Naturally, for this to be possible, the community's director must be secure enough himself to
adapt to such an open structure. He should thus
be trained in group work and should appreciate
the value of this kind of interdisciplinary
approach to treatment.

Ideally, staff members in a TC will reach the point where they no longer think of themselves strictly as nurses, social workers, or psychologists, but transcend professional provincialism with loyalty to the treatment community. This is easier said than accomplished, however. Staff members, like patients, differ widely in their capacity for adapting to and taking part in new therapeutic approaches. Accordingly, while some members might react enthusiastically to the TC's demand for personal and group involvement, others may draw back from it. This is one reason why the TC's director must be proficient in group therapy techniques, and why the staff review is so important.

One criticism that has been leveled at the TC is that its staff may spend more time discussing their own problems than those of the patients they are supposed to be treating. Yet, if staff members are not sensitive to their own needs and abilities, they will be ineffective in their work with others.

Social Learning

The community and staff meetings, then, give every member of the TC an opportunity to analyze his own behavior in a social setting. This is what Jones calls a "living-learning" situation. Living-learning experiences require that participants confront interpersonal problems directly and open themselves to feedback from the group about their strengths and weaknesses. The information gained from such a discussion should help members to face life's difficulties maturely in the future.

However, though the living-learning concept is not a complex one, it can be difficult to carry out. As Jones recognized, "there is an inherent resistance in human beings to examine and discuss what they are doing and why they are doing it." When they are expected not only to analyze their and others' behavior but also to adapt it to the

Therapeutic Community, Guided Group

best interests of the community, this natural
inertia can be hard to overcome.[4]

Crisis situations. When a living-learning
experience is also accompanied by violent emotion,
it is appropriately termed a "crisis situation."
The developers of the TC designed a procedure to
resolve such crises in a manner that would also
encourage the personal growth of the patients and
staff concerned. According to Jones, calming
down a crisis situation involves six elements:
face-to-face confrontation, timing, skilled neutral leadership, open communication, an appropriate level of feeling, and attitudes conducive
to the participants' growth.[5]

We know that people often distort reality
even in average, daily personal interactions. In
emotionally keyed situations, participants and
observers react even more subjectively. To keep
emotions in a negative interpersonal encounter
as controlled as possible, the TC staff attempts
to get those involved in the difficulty to confront each other as soon after the crisis as they
are calm enough to do so. A trained leader helps
them to analyze their confrontation and try to
see how and why it happened. The participants
must feel free to be open, even with their anger
and hostility, so that they can reach an understanding of the problems involved. Then they may
be able to consider making changes in their
behavior.

A crisis is no easier to cool off in a TC
than in a traditional institution, but the method
of handling the problem in a TC often can produce
positive results out of an initially unpleasant
occurrence. If the staff and patients sincerely
want to make it work, and the leader is well-
trained and capable in group interaction, a

[4]Maxwell Jones, Beyond the Therapeutic Community,
Yale University Press, New Haven, Conn., 1968, p. 87.

[5]Ibid., pp. 76-78.

crisis situation can be a positive learning experience for everyone involved.

   Training. In the therapeutic community training is continuous. Formal seminars and sensitivity sessions are held as often as possible but the bulk of the training for both staff and patients is informal. This constant process includes participating in living-learning and crisis situations, as well as being involved in the myriad of other activities that make up the work day in a TC. Since conflicts and crises that arise within the TC are viewed positively as opportunities for treatment and teaching, the therapeutic community is geared to be an unending educational experience for all its members.

   Ideally, this training enables every TC staff member to take a leadership role. As a leader, each one must be sensitive to the needs and capacities of others, be able to motivate people and draw them together, and instill in others the desire to study themselves as a route to achieving personal flexibility. Clearly, then, constant and effective training for the staff is of great importance to the TC.

Therapeutic Community in the Penal Setting

   The concept of the therapeutic community, born shortly after World War II, came at a time when correction systems were ready for liberal reform. They needed a type of treatment that would attend to the social functioning of the inmate, not just his "intrapsychic" activity. The TC seemed to be a likely candidate to fill this void, since it emphasized a fresh environmental approach. Yet, the therapeutic community, in its contemporary form, was not applied in the penal setting to any significant extent until the 1960's.

   One of the most thorough of the early studies on the correctional therapeutic community was done between 1964 and 1966, at the National Institute

41

of Mental Health Research Center in Texas. It
involved thirty prisoners who were drug addicts.
The program directors had found this group to be
particularly resistant to traditional therapy.
As in many prisons, the inmates had developed
cliques which based much of their group solidar-
ity on reacting negatively to certain staff
members.

To change the anti-staff focus of these
prisoner cliques, the directors had to break down
the social walls separating prisoners from staff.
For a start, this meant changing staff attitudes
and stereotypes. The directors then began to
give inmate subgroups more decision-making power,
so that their energies could be directed toward
helping fellow inmates rather than against the
staff. One of these new responsibilities was the
authority to deal with deviant behavior such as
acting out or stealing from other patients, a
role formerly claimed solely by the staff.
Inmates and staff also began to participate
together in community meetings. These changes
improved communication between staff and inmates
considerably, and the community's rehabilitative
program showed noticeably greater success.[6]

Another extensive study of the applicability
of TC concepts in penal institutions was done at
Dannamora, New York, in the Clinton Diagnostic
and Treatment Center. This is a prerelease, pre-
parole maximum security institution in which
inmates stay an average of 12 months. When the
project was initiated in 1966, it treated 50
inmates; it is now up to 100. The average inmate
at Dannamora is an older recidivist who is the
product of an earlier environment that did not
successfully teach him to adjust to a free
society; he is not antisocial.

[6]H. Hughes et al., "Organizing the therapeutic
potential of the addict prisoner community," International
Journal of the Addictions, New York, 5 (2), 1970, pp. 205-
223.

One of the main problems facing the workers at Clinton was the offenders' distrust of figures of authority. On the other hand, the need for staff members to become part of the therapy milieu was counterbalanced by the need for them to remain strong enough authority figures to maintain adequate security.

Unlike the hospital TC, this correctional community makes attendance at treatment sessions compulsory. Directors of the program take advantage of the controlled penal environment in the hope that inmates will begin to accept change through constant contact with, and some degree of involvement in, the treatment process. Clinton's results have been encouraging, though they are not completely conclusive. Essentially, the institution has reached a stage where its center is considered minimum security while the perimeter is operated on a maximum security basis.

Clinton differs significantly from other prisons in the role of its professional correction officers. In Clinton, those in charge of rehabilitation try to utilize the C.O. as fully as possible in several different ways. Not only does he help maintain security and discipline, he is also an important part of the treatment staff. He receives training in TC principles, takes part in therapeutic groups, and contributes to a general atmosphere of freedom in the facility. The Clinton experiment has thus brought the C.O. into the mainstream of the therapeutic community. This achievement may prove to be its greatest contribution to correctional psychology.[7]

Another experiment with TC concepts was undertaken in the '60's at Patuxent Institution, an adult, maximum security prison in Maryland. Researchers at Patuxent decided to study the relationship between the TC and the prison code

[7]Theodore D. Efthihiades and Ludwig Fink, "A study regarding the value of psychotherapy in prison," Criminologica, 6 (1), 1968, pp. 50-56.

of behavior. They arranged the tiers or cell blocks so that each higher level would constitute a more therapeutic environment. The researchers felt that if the TC were effective, the inmates in the highest level would show better social adjustment as the program progressed than those in lower levels. Moreover, those in the lower levels would adhere more closely to the inmate code of prison behavior. This hypothesis was apparently borne out by the results of the study.[8]

The real test of the effectiveness of the TC came when it was used with antisocial patients. Any method that can succeed with this type of criminal population is a noteworthy one, since psychiatrists generally consider this group to be the most incorrigible. The antisocial inmate seems to be amoral; he is difficult to affect with any type of traditional psychotherapeutic treatment since his conscience operates at a different level than a normal individual's.

In a study Agnes Miles conducted in Britain, investigators observed the changes in interpersonal relations of a group of antisocial persons over a period of one year in a TC. Four specific areas were used as criteria of the patient's improvement: acceptance and rejection of peers, formation of friendships and degree of reciprocity in choices of friends, formation of informal friendship groups, and leadership ability. According to Miles, the TC did increase patients' acceptance of peers more effectively than traditional hospital treatment had done with similar groups. Positive results were also reported in the formation of friendships and friendship groups, and the emergence of patient leaders.[9]

[8]John M. Wilson and Jon D. Snodgrass, "The prison code in a therapeutic community," Journal of Criminal Law, Criminology and Police Science, 60 (4), 1969, pp. 472-478.

[9]Agnes Eva Miles, "The effects of a therapeutic community on the interpersonal relationships of a group of psychopaths," British Journal of Criminology, 9 (1), 1969, pp. 22-38.

Another study of antisocial personalities in a British TC involved 122 subjects. The results of this study indicated an improvement rate of 40.1 percent in terms of no further convictions or psychiatric admissions in a two-year period. Of the 87 inmates with a previous history of convictions, 38 (43.6%) had not been reconvicted in the two years after their release; of the 66 with a history of prior psychiatric hospital admission, 38 (57.5%) had not been readmitted in two years.

Despite these relatively positive results, however, researchers did note that the TC was not particularly effective with immature patients who cannot control their impulses or aggressive tendencies. In addition, it had almost no effect on the totally self-centered, impulsive patient whose thought patterns are disorganized—that is, the aggressive antisocial patient. The TC, according to Whitely, is only advisable for those antisocial persons who are not grossly immature and who seem to have potential for growth. [10]

If this is correct, the TC's effectiveness in the penal setting may be limited to young offenders of average intelligence who show potential for change.

Although it is too soon to make a complete evaluation of how much the therapeutic community can contribute to corrections, several points already have become evident: (1) the TC has made some progress in bridging the gap in communication between inmates and staff; (2) trying to institute a TC, with its emphasis on permissiveness, in a prison setting, where control is crucial, can be difficult; (3) since the TC brings out the complete resources of its members by creating an atmosphere that encourages each

[10] J. Stuart Whitely, "The response of psychopaths to a therapeutic community," British Journal of Psychiatry, 116 (534), 1970, pp. 517-529.

participant's feelings of autonomy and self-
respect, there is a risk of occasional disorder.
Accordingly, although the TC has much to offer
correctional psychology, it asks a great deal in
return to make it work.

The TC also requires a great deal of staff
effort to treat small numbers of offenders, and
places a considerable strain on both staff and
patients. Unless inmates are motivated or
coerced into actively participating, and staff
members are willing and able to involve themselves in a community with their charges, the TC
is doomed to failure. Even when the TC seems to
be succeeding, it still may experience periodic
lulls or fail altogether with some inmates.[11]
Moreover, the constraints imposed by the rigid
psychological and physical architecture of most
prisons are bound to limit the TC's use in traditional correctional facilities.

GUIDED GROUP INTERACTION

Correctional psychologists in most penal
centers throughout the world consider group
therapy a logical treatment approach. Not only
does it conserve personnel, it also appears to be
effective with the most difficult offenders—drug
addicts.[12]

Group Work

According to one study, group work seems more
successful than individual therapy at breaking
down the defenses and calming the anxiety of

[11] Loren H. Crabtree and James J. D. Fox, "The overthrow of a therapeutic community," International Journal of
Group Psychotherapy, XXII (1), 1972, pp. 31-41.

[12] Richard W. Nice, "Treatment of the incarcerated
drug user," American Journal of Correction, 33 (1), 1971,
pp. 27-30.

adolescent delinquents being confronted with their personal inadequacies.[13] Therapy groups also appear to be as malleable as individual techniques, since they have been used successfully by group leaders from varied backgrounds in a myriad of settings. Group methods are applicable in a paramilitary structure, or in an unstructured environment. (In an experiment on the West Coast of the United States, chronic traffic violators were treated in an unstructured corrective group.)[14]

Difficulties with Group Therapy

The use of group techniques has increased tremendously in the past decade, to the point that the demand for trained and experienced personnel is exceeding the supply—ironic, considering that one of the intended advantages of the approach is manpower conservation. In fact, the increasing use of group methods in penal settings in some cases inadvertently lowered the professional level and quality of the treatment process. Because of the pressure on treatment staffs to increase the number of inmates participating in groups, many untrained nonprofessionals are conducting groups; the sizes of individual groups have grown to unmanageable proportions; and most sessions merely repress or inspire inmates rather than help them solve their problems.

Another problem with group therapy, which has been glossed over to a large degree, is that it can be potentially harmful as well as beneficial. According to a report released in 1970, delinquents who have fairly strong egos, are socially assertive, and seem to be relatively perceptive may react favorably to intensive group treatment—

[13] Jaime Lievano, "Group psychotherapy with adolescents in an industrial school for delinquent boys," Adolescence, 5 (18), 1970, pp. 231-253.

[14] Robert Bresford, "Group therapy for chronic violators," Trial, 7 (2), 1971, p. 42.

47

however, others may not. Delinquents who tend to retreat from their problems and are easily threatened may be alienated and react defensively.[15]

The use of untrained, poorly supervised non-professionals to conduct group sessions is one of the most blatant—and dangerous—examples of "sugar-coated," do-nothing corrections. On paper, the numerous therapy groups being held seem proof of significant rehabilitative efforts. In reality, most of the groups listed, which might be effective if their paraprofessional leaders were trained and supervised properly, are actually ineffectual, or in some cases even harmful. When nonprofessionals suddenly become group leaders without prior training, the paraprofessional movement is undermined. Furthermore, inmates in these groups do not receive needed treatment, but are left to destroy the groups with their own devices.

Guidelines in group work. Group therapy should by no means be abandoned, however. There is substantial evidence that group work can be quite successful if the group leaders are properly trained. A leader should be able to guide discussions whenever necessary. In providing continuity to the group, however, he should not become its focal point. When advisable, the leader should clarify the group's understanding of issues and behavior. To prevent meetings from degenerating into "gripe sessions," he may need to shift attention from inmates' complaints to the complainers themselves, confronting them with their personal problems, feelings, and viewpoints. The leader should keep the group's goals concrete and within reach; these goals may include provoking and evaluating reactions and adaptations on the part of the institution.[16]

[15] California Youth Authority, The Marshall program: assessment of a short-term institutional program. Part II: Amenability to confrontive peer-group treatment, by Doug Knight, Sacramento, 1970 (Research report no. 59).

[16] Merrit Gilman and Elizabeth Gorlich, Group Counseling with Delinquent Youth (Children's Bureau Publ. No. 459),

Although not every group therapy philosophy
includes all of these guidelines, most group
therapists rely on at least some elements of them.

Group therapy and counseling, then, are often
successful in treating offenders when a trained
leader guides each session. In addition to the
achievements already cited, groups have been
effectively used with sex offenders,[17] with
institutionalized Air Force offenders,[18] and as a
method to relieve prisoner tensions, by opening
the lines of communication, to lessen the problem
of inmate control.[19] Today, the validity of the

U.S. Department of Health, Education, and Welfare, Washing-
ton, D.C., 1968. Also, Gerald J. Forthun and Ronald
Neuhring, "Group work in a maximum security prison," An
Occasional Paper of the School of Social Work (No. 6),
University of Wisconsin, 1968, pp. 9-18.

[17] Amorette Lee Freese, "Group therapy with exhibitionists and voyeurs," Social Work, 17 (2), 1972, pp. 44-52.
Also, Joseph J. Peters and Robert L. Sadoff, "Psychiatric
services for sex offenders on probation," Federal Probation, 35 (3), 1971), pp. 33-37.

[18] Thomas W. Keefe and Thomas H. Smith, "A group coun-
selling and group counselor training program in an Air
Force corrections setting," Corrective Psychiatry and
Journal of Social Therapy, 16 (1,2,3,4), 1970, pp. 97-102.
Also, John Breeskin, "The airmen's readjustment group
therapy program," Corrective Psychiatry and Journal of
Social Therapy, 16 (1,2,3,4), 1970, pp. 103-113. Also,
Thomas J. Foley, Jr., "The efficiency of group psycho-
therapy with first-term airmen at an Air Force Technical
Training Center," Corrective Psychiatry and Journal of
Social Therapy, 16 (1,2,3,4), 1970, pp. 46-50.

[19] Lorraine I. Davis and Katherine B. Kaminski, "The
use of groups at a training school for delinquent girls,"
An Occasional Paper of the School of Social Work (No. 6),
University of Wisconsin, 1968, pp. 1-8. Also, Frank
Shavlik, Institutional Community Interpersonal Relations
Project: Final Report, Federal Reformatory, El Reno,
Oklahoma, 1970.

group approach is not seriously questioned. It is the abilities of those conducting the sessions, the types of populations being treated, and the specific group techniques employed that are being examined.

Guided Group Interaction

One of these group techniques, specially tailored for use in correctional rehabilitation, is Guided Group Interaction (GGI). It was introduced in New Jersey, shortly after World War II.

Like reality therapy, GGI rejects the concept of mental illness as the reason for most abnormal behavior. In this respect it is within the mainstream of much of today's thinking in psychology. Proponents of GGI believe that the group leader should be active and involved in the sessions, especially at first. They feel that free, frank discussion between patients and group leader and among patients is a central method of reeducation: Each patient's fellow deviants are agents for change. The object of GGI sessions is to provide members with enough information, understanding, and motivation to adapt to society.

In becoming involved in GGI the individual usually goes through several stages: At first he is guarded, as his defenses begin to weaken. With encouragement from the leader and support from the other members, he learns to give up the games and defenses he has used in the past to deal with the world.

At the second stage, the inmate's problems with interpersonal relationships are brought into the open. He is encouraged to talk about himself and his values are evaluated, reflected, and challenged by the group.

At the third stage, the prisoner examines the difficulties he has had with his environment. As trust builds up among the group members, they begin to relate and discuss the problems of institutional and street living.

At the fourth stage, the confinee feels
secure and accepts reeducation. As he begins to
realize that his problems are not unique and that
it is possible to deal with them, he feels less
antagonistic toward the group and views their
comments more objectively than before.

Finally, the inmate sets up an outline of a
plan to change. He makes a conscious decision
about the behavior he will follow in the future,
growing out of his own and the group's continual
reexamination of him.

Applications of GGI

Guided Group Interaction was originally used
with youthful first offenders in what was known
as the Highfields Project in New Jersey. The
participants were delinquent youths on probation.
They lived at the project and worked during the
day; the sessions were held at night. GGI concepts permeated all aspects of their environment. In the group session and during the rest
of his waking hours, each member was expected to
be honest, to help others with their problems,
and to confront his own deviant methods of behaving, both on his own and when forcibly faced with
reality by his peers.[20]

The success of the Highfields experiment led
to others. Walton Village has implemented a
modified version of GGI,[21] and the technique also
received wide acceptance in Florida and Minnesota.[22] Since 1969, the Florida Division of Youth

[20] Lloyd McCorkle, The Highfields Story, Holt, Rinehart & Winston, New York, 1958.

[21] Eugene J. Montone, "Walton Village: a modified
guided group interaction approach," Quarterly, 24 (3),
1967, pp. 16-22.

[22] Charles Larson, Guided Group Interaction: Theory
and Method, Hennepin County (Minn.) Court Services Department, Minneapolis, 1970.

Services has been using Guided Group Interaction in all of its institutions. The group is usually made up of 10-12 youths living together in a cottage. Its leader may be a teacher, house-parent, secretary, social worker, or even one of the maintenance crew. Meetings are open and are handled by the inmates after a preliminary state-ment by the group leader. The group itself decides what topic and person will be focused on during each session.

Difficulties with GGI

Guided Group Interaction is considered to be "highly effective" by some investigators.[23] How-ever, at least one reviewer of the GGI process, though favorably impressed with it, expressed some caution. According to George Vold,

The experiment in Guided Group Interaction must face two basic, critical questions:

1. Is it a technique that can be adminis-tered by ordinary individuals after suitable training, or is it a non-specific influence that depends for success on a particular personality?

2. Is it a technique that shows lasting effects in careful comparison with non-guided "control groups" carefully matched for accurate comparison?[24]

Though Vold's comments seem to be general to the point of being trite, they do contain an element of importance that bears watching. Can strong friendships, camaraderie, and healthy family life be created and continually renewed in the face of the rapid turnover of staff and

[23] Albert Elias, "Group treatment program for juvenile delinquents," Child Welfare, 47 (5), 1968, pp. 281-290.

[24] George B. Vold, "Discussion," American Sociologi-cal Review, 16, 1959, p. 460.

inmates inherent in correctional institutions?
Is GGI really significantly more effective than
other forms of group therapy? Does the process
itself produce success, or is the person leading
the group the deciding factor? These questions
must be considered.

From the positive reports already in on GGI,
as well as the acceptance it has gained in
certain penal systems, it must be considered
successful. However, as Vold noted, we must be
careful not to accept GGI as more effective than
other methods of group therapy until it has been
tested still further.

CORE REFERENCES

Therapeutic Community

Jones, Maxwell. <u>Social Psychiatry in Prac-
tice</u>. Baltimore: Penguin Books, 1968.
A succinct examination of the TC concept.

Crabtree, Loren, and Fox, James. "The overthrow of a therapeutic community," <u>International
Journal of Group Psychotherapy</u>, XXII (1), 1972,
pp. 31-41.
An illustration of the problems that can
arise when a TC is being set up.

Group Work in the Correctional Setting

Fenton, Norman. <u>An Introduction to Group
Counseling in Correctional Service</u>. Washington,
D.C.: American Correction Association, 1957.
A relatively good introduction to group
counseling in corrections.

Guided Group Interaction

McCorkle, Lloyd, Elise, Albert, and Bixby,
Lorrell. <u>The Highfields Story</u>. New York: Henry
Holt & Co., 1958.
A thorough presentation of a correctional
setting that uses GGI.

Larson, Charles. <u>Guided Group Interaction</u>:
<u>Theory and Method</u>. Minneapolis: Hennepin County
(Minn.) Court Services Department, 1970.
A good overview of the GGI process.

CHAPTER 4

Behavior
Modification

To many people, the idea of behavior control technology suggests futuristic humanoids, thought
restriction, and activity monitoring. Even those
who are not actually frightened by news of techniques designed to shape behavior seem to be concerned about how these techniques might be used.

In fact, however, behavior shaping has been
tremendously valuable as a method of treating
psychological disorders. The early learning
experiments performed by such theorists as Pavlov,
Hull, and Skinner have led behavioral scientists
far beyond the laboratory. Today, research and
experiments continue to build on the work of those
early pioneers to produce successful techniques
of behavior modification.

BEHAVIOR MODIFICATION

Behavior therapists consider the goals of
therapeutic intervention and the aims of learning
principles to be the same—that is, the alteration
of behavior. The behaviorist, feeling that antisocial behavior is learned and that learning is
the result of reinforced practice, believes
relearning can replace undesirable behavior

patterns with acceptable ones. Essentially, the strategy of behavioristic techniques is to analyze behavior in terms of a pattern of stimuli in the environment causing responses in the subjects. By discovering which stimuli will elicit what response (usually taken to be a symptom or some form of undesirable behavior), either the stimuli can be eliminated or a new competing response can be conditioned to the old stimuli. Thus, in either event the undesirable behavior is eliminated.[1]

Two Forms of Behavior Therapy

Pavlov's <u>respondent conditioning</u> and Skinner's <u>operant</u> version were the forerunners of two distinct behavioristic schools. Following the lead of the Russian physiologist Pavlov, investigators such as Wolpe and Eysenck pioneered the respondent form of behavior therapy. One technique often used in this approach is <u>systematized desensitization</u>. The following steps illustrate how this method would be used with a phobia (irrational fear):

1. The subject is extensively interviewed to determine his stimuli hierarchy; that is, what stimuli provoke the most and the least anxiety in the subject.

2. The psychologist uses techniques of suggestion or hypnosis to induce the patient to relax.

3. Anxiety-provoking stimuli are presented to the subject while he is relaxed. The least threatening stimulus is presented first, and the therapist moves up the scale at a pace acceptable to the patient.

This form of <u>counterconditioning</u>, in which the therapist reduces or inhibits the patient's response to an anxiety-provoking stimulus by

[1]Helen Lantz and Gilbert Ingram, "The psychopath and his response to behavior modification techniques," <u>FCI Technical and Treatment Notes</u>, 2 (1), 1971, pp. 7-8.

pairing it with a neutral stimulus (his relaxed state), has been extremely effective. However, it is not the only form of behavior therapy. In contrast to those who built their therapeutic approach on the classical respondent conditioning model set up by Pavlov, four other methods were derived from the operant or instrumental conditioning technique studied and advanced by Skinner. These four methods involve encouraging a desired response to a stimulus by rewarding it either with a positive reinforcer or with the elimination of a negative reinforcer. The four methods can be broken down as follows:

A. To eliminate a response:

1. Omission training: An undesirable response is not followed by a positive reinforcer (reward).

2. Punishment training: An undesirable response is followed by a negative reinforcer (for example, pain).

B. To aid or increase the frequency of a response:

3. Avoidance training: A desired response is followed by an opportunity to avoid a negative reinforcer (such as an electric shock).

4. Reward training: A desired response is followed by a positive reinforcer (for example, money).

To summarize, then, the behavior therapist of the operant school has two general aims: (1) to reinforce desirable behavior by rewarding it, or by removing a negative stimulus, and (2) to extinguish undesirable behavior by not rewarding it, or by punishing it with a negative stimulus. Like the respondent school, the operant one has been quite successful in applying learning concepts to replace undesirable responses with acceptable ones.

BEHAVIOR MODIFICATION AND THE OFFENDER

Behavioral scientists have conducted a number of studies to determine whether delinquent behavior is learned or may result from an inherited predisposition (XYY syndrome). Although some criminals do show chromosomal abnormalities, those few offenders with this genetic peculiarity generally have been abnormally asocial, aggressive, and resistant to therapy.[2] Most theorists agree that the problems of the bulk of the criminal population are environmental, not genetic.

The "average" offender, then, has learned the inappropriate ways in which he responds to the demands of his environment. Therefore, rehabilitation should correct his undesirable behavior by means of shaping procedures. Shaping, in this sense, refers to altering a pattern of behavior by reinforcing responses that resemble the ones desired. Successive rewards are given as the responses come closer and closer to the goal behavior until it is finally achieved.

Unfortunately, an ironic block to effective behavioral treatment is the fact that the delinquent's peer group often runs a more efficient behavior modification program than the prison staff, even though they are not familiar with the theory behind their actions. Therapists sometimes postpone rewards and punishments, or apply them inconsistently; but offenders are quick to

[2] W. H. Price, J. A. Strong, P. B. Whatmore, and W. F. McClemont, "Criminal patients with XYY sex-chromosome complement," Lancet, 1, 1966, pp. 565-566. Also, H. Hunter, "Klinefelter's syndrome and delinquency," British Journal of Criminology, 8, 1968, pp. 203-207. Also, J. Nielson, "The XYY syndrome in a mental hospital: genetically determined criminality," British Journal of Criminology, 8, 1968, pp. 186-203. Also, P. A. Jacobs, M. Brunton, M. M. Melvill, R. P. Brittain, and W. F. McClemont, "Aggressive behavior, mental sub-normality and the XYY male," Nature, 208, 1965, pp. 1351-1352.

punish moves by the inmate toward socially acceptable behavior, and never stop verbally supporting
antisocial behavior. Some institutions have taken
steps to correct this problem by strengthening the
staff's competence with behavioral techniques.
These steps include ensuring that institutional
personnel adhere to a rigorous behavioral approach
and apply tailor-made schedules of reward and
punishment; and closely observing the ways inmates
use positive and negative reinforcement.[3]

Behavior Modification in
Penal Institutions

Techniques of shaping behavior in prisons
have progressed by now to a point where expectations for them are high. Many psychologists
continue to experiment with behavior modification
to test the limits of its value in the correctional setting.

In one experiment, researchers used behavior
modification principles to try to improve inmates'
records of keeping their appointments with their
staff psychologists. The positive reinforcement
was the therapist's expression of general approval
when an inmate showed up for his appointment,
whether he was prompt or tardy. The negative
reinforcement was the psychologist's disapproval
when the subject's attendance was poor.

This study seemed to bear out the applicability of behavior modification to appointment-
keeping behavior, for which it claimed significant
improvement. It also appeared to have a further
implication: It apparently encouraged promptness,
which is a requirement of society in employment,
school, and other areas. Accordingly, the study
not only improved the inmates' institutional

[3] R. E. Buehler, G. R. Patterson, and J. M. Furniss,
"The reinforcement of behavior in institutional settings,"
Behavior Research and Therapy, 4, 1966, pp. 157-167.

behavior, but also theoretically helped them pre-pare to return to the community.[4]

Behavior modification also shows promise of being one of the more economical programs for penal institutions in terms of time, money, and effort. In addition, modification methods may be useful in treating self-injurious behavior, and in keeping down the number of escapes, riots, and prison disturbances.[5] The study of correctional behavior modification has also cast a new light on the value of punishment. Since Enrico Ferri's research at the end of the nineteenth century, many psychologists and sociologists have reached the conclusion that punishment alone is probably relatively ineffective in bringing about lasting change in behavioral patterns.[6] The type of haphazard, low-intensity punishment meted out in most correctional facilities does not carry the impact of the immediate, brief, high-intensity type, given along with an alternate behavioral choice.

[4]Gary White Hanson, "Behavior modification of appoint-ment attendance among youthful offenders," FCI Research Reports, 3 (2), 1971.

[5]Michael Hindelang, "A learning theory analysis of the correctional process," Issues in Criminology, 5 (1), 1970, pp. 43-59. Also, Nathan B. Miron, "Behavior modifi-cation techniques in the treatment of self-injurious behavior in institutionalized retardates," Bulletin of Suicidology, No. 8, U.S. Government Printing Office, 1971, pp. 64-69. Also, R. McCaldon et al., "Forensic seminar on reward and punishment," Canadian Journal of Corrections, 12 (1), 1970, pp. 25-39.

[6]H. C. Hutchison, "Behaviour theory, behaviour science and treatment," Canadian Journal of Corrections, 10 (2), 1968, pp. 388-391. Also, Pran Chopra, "Punishment and the control of human behavior," Australian and New Zealand Journal of Criminology, 2 (3), 1969, pp. 149-157.

Possibly the most important finding by investigators of behavioral modification in the prison setting is the recognition of the need to include the line correction officer (C.O.) in the treatment team. As staff-inmate ratios improve with the influx of new personnel, the C.O., whose role is broadening to include rehabilitation responsibilities, will be expected to maintain more constant contact with the inmate. As a result, he will be required to deal effectively with a myriad of behavioral problems. He will need to be aware of the importance of reinforcing appropriate behavior so its frequency will increase. Likewise, he will need to understand the necessity to ignore inappropriate behavior as much as is realistically possible, so it will decrease and eventually disappear once it is no longer reinforced by attention. In essence, he will have to be able to examine the institutional environment, consider the alternatives available within its framework, and utilize them to influence inmate behavior.[7]

THE TOKEN ECONOMY

The use of behavior modification techniques in corrections is not really new. Token economies, where inmates earn or lose points by behaving acceptably or unacceptably, date back to the early 1800's and have been used in a variety of correctional settings. One of the first to introduce such a "mark philosophy" was the penal colony at Norfolk Island, Sydney, Australia. Under the supervision of Alexander Maconochie, a positive, constructive substitute for corporal punishment was introduced. Each prisoner forfeited marks, which prolonged his confinement, instead of receiving physical punishment. When a prisoner earned a certain number of marks by good behavior, he won his

[7]Richard C. Pooley, The control of human behavior in a correctional setting, Center for the Study of Crime, Delinquency and Corrections, 1969.

liberty. Goods and services could also be "purchased" with the marks. The supervisor kept a strict record of each inmate's marks.

Spike Island, Ireland, was another penal setting that pioneered the application of behavior modification techniques. Under the Irish Progressive Stage Systems of Corrections employed on Spike Island, a prisoner could improve his living accommodations, work assignments, and amount of leisure time as he advanced from Stage One to Stage Four. The first stage consisted of solitary confinement, reduced diet, and some monotonous work (picking oakum). The prisoner could progress to more interesting work, some education, and better treatment during the latter part of this first stage. Stage Two consisted of assignment to public works at Spike Island; the inmate's privileges also increased at this point. Stage Three included some work without supervision, and Stage Four was a form of probation.

Robert F. Kennedy Youth Center, in Morgantown, West Virginia, is a recent example of a correctional setting that extensively employs behavior modification techniques. At RFK Youth Center, reinforcement strategies are built into almost every student activity; both a class level system and a token economy are in use.

The class level system has proved to be one of the institution's most highly effective motivators of good behavior. By achieving progressively higher goals set by the cottage committee, youths can earn advancement from Trainee to Apprentice to Honor Student. Living accommodations, work assignments, pay, clothing, and recreation improve with each class level.

Students usually progress from Trainee to Apprentice in 3 to 5 months and reach Honor status in from 5 to 8 months. They usually are ready for release in 10 to 12 months.

A second major reinforcer of positive
behavior is the token economy system. While
this approach to retraining has been used
successfully in other areas (mental health,
retardation, emotional disturbance), its
application in corrections has been limited.
Consequently, its institution-wide use at
the Center represents one of the more ambitious undertakings of this nature in the
field of corrections to date.

Under the token economy, students earn points
(1 point equals 1 cent) as they meet goals
set in each program area (school, work,
cottage life). The students use the points
to "buy" a wide variety of goods and services
available at the institution.

Each youth receives a weekly pay check, in
points, based on staff ratings of his daily
performance. Their pay check again reflects
the distinction made between class levels.
Apprentices earn points at a rate higher than
Trainee and Honor students earn at a rate
higher than Apprentices. A student also may
earn "bonus" points, awarded on the spot for
certain kinds of positive behavior.

A student's institution expenses, including
room rent, are deducted from his pay check.
Trainees pay the least and Apprentices and
Honor students pay more for their more
desirable quarters. Fines, which are few,
also are deducted from the pay check. Here,
again, discipline is differentiated. . . .
A fine for an Honor student may be up to
three times that assessed a Trainee.

Students also can use their points to buy
commissary, snack bar goods, and civilian
clothing, and to participate in recreational
activities. Points are not transferable
from one student to another. They can spend
only what they themselves earn. In effect,

the point system teaches youths that if they want something they must work for it.[8]

The comprehensive program of the RFK Youth Center, which utilizes both a class level system and a token economy, merits watching. As RFK is probably one of the most ambitious recent attempts to apply behavior modification techniques in corrections, its failures as well as its successes will help provide a direction for correctional psychologists in the future.

In another study, J. Burchard and Vernon Tyler subjected a 13-year-old delinquent's anti-social behavior to operant conditioning. This boy had been institutionalized from the age of nine because his mother was unable to control his destructive and disruptive behavior—cruelty to small children and animals, setting fires, and stealing. Traditional therapy seemed to have no significant effect on him.

When the researchers examined the youngster's environment at the institution, they found that his surroundings seemed to maintain rather than discourage his antisocial behavior. The punishment he received (isolation in his room) actually reinforced the undesirable actions it was supposed to deter. While in his room he received attention from his peers, and pity—as well as occasional snacks—from some of the staff.

The first step in applying operant conditioning to this case was, of course, to stop these rewards. Any time the boy was put into isolation, the researchers ensured that this punishment would not be a vehicle for increased attention. In addition, he was given tokens as a reward for good behavior, which he could redeem for canteen goods, recreational materials, and other things he wanted. After five months of this treatment, his

[8]Roy Gerard, "Institutional innovations in juvenile corrections," Federal Probation, 1970.

behavior had improved enough for him to be housed in an open cottage.[9]

The use of financial incentives or tokens seems to be quite a successful technique for changing undesirable response patterns in prisoners. Moreover, behavioral techniques have achieved positive results in the community as well as in correctional institutions.

Token Reinforcement in the Community

Elery Phillips' work with predelinquent boys was one experiment that demonstrated how token reinforcement procedures could modify the behavior of youths in a community-based, home-style reha- bilitative environment. "Predelinquents" are children whose disruptive behavior in their home setting indicates that they are liable to have trouble with the law in the future. The tokens in Phillips' study were given out by the house parents, and were distributed or taken away depending on the youths' behavior.

The target or desired behavior patterns involved social, self-care, and academic areas considered to be important for the youth's devel- opment. Tokens were administered as points, and were noted on 3x5" index cards which the boys always carried. Points earned or lost were posted immediately after the behavior that was responsible for them was observed, maintaining a prompt reinforcement schedule.

Points were tallied at the end of each week to determine privileges for the next week. Some of the privileges, and the points required for them, were allowance (1000), games (500), and permission to come home late after school (1000). Typical activities that would earn a boy points redeemable for privileges were reading books

[9]J. Burchard and Vernon Tyler, Jr., "The modification of delinquent behavior through operant conditioning," Behavior Research and Therapy, 2, 1965, pp. 245-250.

Behavior Modification

(5-10 per page), washing dishes (500-1000 per
meal), and cleaning and maintaining one's room
(500 per day).

The youths could also lose points for certain
actions. Some behaviors that lost them points
were speaking aggressively (20-50 points per
response), arguing (30 points per response), and
stealing, lying, or cheating (10,000 per response).

Phillips concluded from this study that a
token reinforcement procedure, entirely dependent
upon the back-up reinforcement naturally available in a home-style setting, could contribute to
an effective and economical rehabilitation program with predelinquents. He reported that the
frequency of aggressive statements and poor
grammar decreased, while tidiness, punctuality,
and amount of homework completed increased.[10]

Though this study was done with predelinquents, such a program could be applied with other
age groups in the community setting as well.
Edward Ray and Kent Kilburn discussed the advantages and disadvantages of such programs and their
implications for probation officers in an article
in Criminology. Unlike institutional behavioral
programs, community-based ones do not have the
advantage of close administrative control. However, this situation is balanced out by several
advantages, such as not having to combat the
rigid, authoritarian, bureaucratic characteristics of many institutions. Furthermore, behavior
acquired in a community program seems more
readily adaptable to real life, since it was
learned where it would eventually be practiced—
in the community.

Ray and Kilburn also noted two implications
for probation officers (P.O.'s) in the large-
scale use of behavior modification techniques in

[10] Elery L. Phillips, "Achievement place: token reinforcement procedures in a home-style setting for 'predelinquent' boys," Journal of Applied Behavior Analysis, 1 (3),
1968, pp. 213-223.

community-based settings. First, the P.O.'s role
would shift from simply counseling to primarily
applying behavioral techniques. This would obviously require additional training. Second, the
P.O.'s would have to be familiar with the
resources available in the community and the
options these resources could provide for inte-
grated programming with other sectors of the
community.[11]

The probation officer is crucial to the
offender's rehabilitation, since he is present at
a time when few other behavior modification
controls are available. Reinforcement schedules
in a community setting are often weak and uncertain, and there are many stressful and disruptive
influences in the community that have been eliminated from the institutional setting.[12] If the
P.O. is prepared to understand and administer the
behavioral system in spite of the obstacles posed
by the unstable community setting, much may be
gained.

Thorne, Tharp, and Wetzel suggest that one
answer to the problem of the P.O.'s lack of
familiarity with behavioral principles is to use
psychologists trained in this area as consultants.
These authors also recommend that the P.O. should
place increased emphasis on positive rewards, not
just punishment, as is traditional in probation.
One case history they gave to illustrate the need
for more use of rewards was especially informative, because it pointed up some of the strengths
and weaknesses of behavior modification techniques when applied by probation officers.

[11] Edward T. Ray and Kent L. Kilburn, "Behavior
modification techniques applied to community behavior
problems," Criminology, 8 (2), 1970, pp. 173-184.

[12] Saleem A. Shah, "Some basic principles and concepts
of behavior modification," in "Conference on the social
restoration of offenders through manpower development and
training," Wakoff Research Center, 1967.

Loren is a 16 year old boy who lives with
his stepfather, mother, and two younger
brothers. He was referred for (1) assaultive
behavior—threatening to shoot his stepfather
and trying to fist fight with both parents;
(2) defiance of nearly all parental requests
(coming home early at night, completing his
household chores, mowing the lawn, not
taking the car without permission); and (3)
habitual truancy. Police had been called
for several of these incidents, and referral
was made from the local juvenile court.

Assessment of the family revealed that Loren
was on an entirely aversive reinforcement
schedule. He was denied allowance,
restricted from the car, continually threatened with the police, and verbally abused.
None of these was effective. Money, use of
the car and nights out were considered positively reinforcing, but the parents were so
angry with Loren they provided no clear way
for him to earn these. An interview with
Loren confirmed the latter.

Loren's parents were where many are at the
point of referral—desperate. They had been
meeting each infraction with punishment until
a point of no return was reached. The
thought of rewarding Loren for approximations
of "good" behavior had not occurred to them
and the suggestion was met with great skepti-
cism. However, since they had exhausted
their own repertoire of controls, the project
staff member was able to persuade them to at
least give his suggestions a try.

Two points in the family assessment were
quite important. First, Loren apparently
had never been given a clear idea of his
parents' expectations. For example, instruc-
tions such as "Be in at a decent hour" made
for much uncertainty. Second, it became
obvious that his stepfather wanted the boy
out of the home and was trying to accomplish
this through unrealistic and vacillating
demands.

68

The intervention plan consisted of a carefully devised schedule—more nearly a contract—which would allow Loren to earn money for completion of chores and being obedient (e.g., on a weekend night he must be in by midnight). Failures brought not only a loss of money but also carried a fine in the form of 15-minute blocks of restricted time from use of the family car. For the first time he knew exactly how to earn money and time away from home, and exactly what the consequences would be for not conforming. The parents were not to hedge on the contingencies, and biweekly phone calls from our staff plus a posted copy of the "contract" were used to prevent this.

Rapid changes subsequently occurred in Loren's behavior. In the first 35 days, he was rewarded an average of 81 percent of the time in each of four areas of responsibility (range 75 to 89 percent). Prior to intervention he met these obligations rarely (0 to 10 percent).

At this point a second contract was drawm up because Loren's stepfather was continuing to nag him despite tremendous improvement and because Loren's car insurance had expired and his stepfather refused to renew it. The new contract was negotiated in the presence of both parents, Loren, and a project staff member. It allowed for points to be earned for chores and responsibilities which could be applied to the car insurance premium (stepfather agreed finally to this). Loren could earn a maximum of 50 points a week, and needed 250 for the premium. The first week he earned 22 points and then the full 50 on each week thereafter.

Loren began driving the car again, but only by meeting specific contingencies agreed to by his parents, himself and staff. In addition, he reentered high school, achieved satisfactorily, was not truant, and had

applied for an after school job. The case
was maintained at this level of success for
24 days, requiring only one phone call to
the parents and two brief home visits.
Loren's stepfather and mother expressed
satisfaction over the changes and felt that
he was doing so well that the "contract"
should be abandoned. Our staff member
vigorously tried to discourage this, feeling
that such a drastic change was premature.
However, the parents persevered and abruptly
ceased abiding by the agreements and contingencies.

Events following the parents' return to pre-
intervention conditions illustrate an unfortunate collapse of environmental controls.
Loren was truant for the succeeding 7 school
days, and was arrested 11 days later for
burglary. His parents refused to visit him
during 2 days at a detention home. In addition, they told the probation officer that
Loren was "hopelessly" bad despite all the
good things they had done for him. The
court placed Loren on probation and reluc-
tantly allowed him to return to his home.
The project had recommended foster placement
but none was available. His adjustment
remains exceedingly tenuous at home, but the
parents refused further help. [13]

Loren's case demonstrates that behavioral
techniques can modify inappropriate behavior by
altering its environmental consequences. But this
example also illustrates how important the coopera-
tion of the parents is. The probation officer
adopting operant techniques will find that parents
unwilling or unable to try the behavioral methods
of reward and punishment during probation can
prevent the approach from succeeding.

[13] Gaylord L. Thorne, Roland G. Tharp, and Ralph J.
Wetzel, "Behavior modification techniques: new tools for
probation officers," Federal Probation, 1967, pp. 21-27.

MODIFYING THE BEHAVIOR OF
ANTISOCIAL OFFENDERS

The antisocial category is one which is extremely resistant to treatment. Since this is the case, this class of offenders would seem to be an ideal testing ground for behavior modification techniques. As Helen Lantz and Gilbert Ingram point out in their behavior modification paper, "The psychopathic personality—undersocialized and asocial—may well be the group of disorders for which the greatest departure from traditional treatment is needed."[14] Of the impressive amount of literature reviewed in the Lantz - Ingram survey of the use of behavior modification techniques with antisocial patients, two of the studies cited are particularly worthy of note.

One of these studies, by J. L. Bernard and R. Eisenman, reported that sociopathic subjects were easier to condition than normal subjects for either social or monetary reinforcement. These authors concluded that sociopaths have learned different values, imitate different models, and follow different patterns of behavior from the rest of the population. Accordingly, instead of being simply unable to learn or otherwise respond to social stimuli, sociopaths fail to learn in some, but not all, situations. In other words, the behavior therapist can effectively treat the sociopath once he finds out what is rewarding for the particular subject he is treating.[15]

Another especially informative study was done by D. N. Painting, who underlined the importance of the immediacy of the reinforcer. If an antisocial individual is not confronted with the

---

[14] Lantz and Ingram, op. cit., p. 8.

[15] J. L. Bernard and R. Eisenman, "Verbal conditioning in sociopaths with social and monetary reinforcement," Journal of Personality and Social Psychology, 6, 1967, pp. 203-206.

consequences of his behavior within a short time, he may not make the connection between his action and its impact, which may even encourage inappropriate behavior. Painting's research indicated that antisocial persons are less capable than others of perceiving relationships between past events and their consequences in the present. In further testing this hypothesis, he also found antisocial patients to be more easily conditioned than others when stimulus and response were in close proximity. As the time between stimulus and response increased, the patients' receptiveness to conditioning rapidly decreased. Behavior modification techniques thus seem to be more effective with antisocial subjects than are other therapeutic measures that do not immediately reinforce target behaviors.[16]

PROBLEMS WITH BEHAVIOR MODIFICATION

Although behavior modification has achieved positive results with juvenile delinquents, probationers, predelinquents, and other classes of offenders—including treatment-resistant antisocial patients—there are still some difficulties with this approach. However, most of the objections to it are leveled at behavioral techniques in general, rather than their specific application in the correctional setting.

Critics of behavior modification have expressed objections for as long as it has been in use. Among their primary criticisms are (1) treating the patient's overt symptoms is too superficial to be effective; (2) the token economy and similar mechanistic approaches cannot change underlying causes of deviant behavior; (3) the effects of behavioristic methods may not be lasting; and (4) behavior modification might cause

[16] D. N. Painting, "Performance of psychopathic individuals under conditions of positive and negative partial reinforcement," Journal of Abnormal and Social Psychology, 62, 1961, pp. 352-355.

symptom substitution—that is, when one behavior is eliminated, another possibly more disturbed symptom may take its place.[17]

To be objective, the professional in the correctional psychology field must give these criticisms respectful study. In addition, we must realize that much of the positive data reported by experimenters in behavior modification is still inconclusive. Nevertheless, behavior modification has already had some indisputable positive impact, and it continues to show promise in corrections. Optimism regarding the use of behavior modification techniques may eventually prove premature, but it is hard to imagine that this treatment strategy will not have some positive role to play in corrections in the future.

CORE REFERENCES

Behavior Modification and the Offender

Lantz, Helen, and Ingram, Gilbert. "The psychopath and his response to behavior modification techniques," FCI Technical and Treatment Notes, 1971, 2 (1).
A discussion of the use of behavior modification with antisocial personalities.

Stumphauzer, J. S. "Behavior modification with juvenile delinquents: a critical review," FCI Technical and Treatment Notes, 1970, 1 (2).
A thorough survey of the use of behavior modification techniques with juvenile delinquents.

[17] Cyril M. Franks, Behavior Therapy, Appraisal and Status, McGraw-Hill, New York, 1969, pp. 3-4.

Behavior Modification

Thorne, Gaylord, Tharp, Roland, and Wetzel, Ralph. "Behavior modification techniques: new tools for probation officers," Federal Probation, 1967, 31 (2).
An introduction to the use of behavior modification techniques in probation.

Behavior Modification

Franks, Cyril (ed.). Behavior Therapy: Appraisal and Status. New York: McGraw-Hill, 1969.
A systematic and comprehensive overview of the field of behavior therapy.

Wolpe, J. "Psychotherapy based on the principle of reciprocal inhibition." In Burton, A. (ed.), Case Studies of Counseling and Psychotherapy. Englewood Cliffs, New Jersey: Prentice-Hall, 1959.
An excellent presentation of how reciprocal inhibition is used as a therapeutic technique.

CHAPTER 5

Nonprofessionals
in Corrections

In today's credential-checking society, sometimes
it seems as though the only legitimate behavioral
therapy is the interaction between a "documented"—
Ph.D., M.D., M.S.W.—professional and a "certified"
patient. In fact, though, people with psychological problems are constantly finding help from
friends that any status-conscious doctor would
consider unqualified. Psychologists' recognition
of this fact, and of the need to organize and
encourage this process on a larger scale, has led
to the much-discussed nonprofessional movement in
mental health.

NONPROFESSIONALS IN THE MENTAL HEALTH FIELD

In a loose sense, the mental health field
could be called the stepfather of modern corrections. New ways of using nonprofessionals in the
mental health discipline, and the rationale underlying these innovations, are being adopted by the
offender treatment field as well.

The uneven quality of the mental health
services available to patients, and the shortage
of manpower to treat them, led to a movement to
train nonprofessionals in the principles of
psychological care. This additional talent could

lessen the pressure on psychiatrists, psychologists, and social workers, and help them expand treatment facilities. In addition, since many of the new people hired would be from the same socioeconomic class as the population they would eventually serve, the patients might be able to understand, identify with, and trust them more readily than professionals. By the same token, a nonprofessional from a background similar to that of his patients might be more sensitive to their racial, educational, social, and economic problems.

Another advantage to the mental health program using paraprofessionals is the economic savings possible. In a progress report on the use of legal paraprofessionals in Pennsylvania, for example, it was conservatively estimated that the program had saved the state's taxpayers more than $300,000 during the first six months of 1972.[1] The nonprofessional movement, therefore, brings to corrections a new hope that the extent and quality of treatment services can be increased at a minimal cost.

The First Steps

As in the mental health area, the correctional nonprofessional (also called a case aide, paraprofessional, or subprofessional) is expected to be able to make and maintain contact with those alienated from the usual sources of service and help. However, if he is supposed to contribute significantly to the treatment process and not serve simply as an errand boy, a number of steps have to be taken to prepare him for his role. Nonprofessionals tossed abruptly into the correctional setting, without any preliminary preparation, may do more harm than good. Instead of welcoming the assistance of new aides, both inmates and surprised professionals may become alarmed on

[1] State Correctional Institution at Graterford, Pennsylvania, The Paraprofessional Law Clinic: Progress Report, Graterford, Pa., 1972.

either practical or self-interest grounds. To improve the chances of the paraprofessional program's success, and to lessen the threat some bureaucratic professionals feel from the entry of nonprofessionals into their field, several preparations are usually made. Imaginative training programs are developed with the aid of the staff professionals; salaried positions are established for the untrained nonprofessionals being hired, and new career ladders are created.[2]

Developing a Training Program

In a discussion of the frustrations of overworked professional correction workers, D. R. Cressey pointed out that ". . . there is no shortage of mature, moral, average, fine . . . men and women of the kind making up the majority of the personnel manning our factories, our businesses, and our prisons—men and women who have a high school education at most."[3] Cressey thus not only touched upon the potential value of nonprofessional help, but indirectly uncovered a difficulty in using this kind of worker as well. Because most paraprofessionals lack an extensive formal education, and are not always receptive to conventional types of teaching, the professional staff must provide innovative training for them. Audiovisual aids, sensitivity sessions, role-playing, or case study presentations can supplement or even replace the traditional lecture sessions. Such devices are particularly useful for covering the areas that nonprofessionals seem to have the most trouble with. These areas include assuming of authority, accepting the need to maintain confidentiality, maintaining a professional attitude, and keeping in touch with the

[2]Arthur Pearl and Frank Riessman, New Careers for the Poor, Free Press, New York, 1965.

[3]D. R. Cressey, "Theoretical foundations for using criminals in the rehabilitation of criminals," Key Issues, 2, 1965, pp. 87-101.

community outside while moving up the organiza-
tional ladder themselves.[4]

Establishing Salaried Positions
for Nonprofessionals

In the past, many health and rehabilitation
organizations found it desirable to open up volunteer positions for nonprofessionals. These jobs
offered the participants training that could eventually be applied toward salaried jobs. However,
an unemployed nonprofessional from a ghetto area
would not be able to afford to take a non-paying
job, and thus such a policy might prevent many
motivated workers from entering the field. As a
result, a number of federal and city programs now
offer salaried positions to nonprofessionals even
when they do not have any training in corrections.
This step has aided the recruitment of talented
paraprofessionals immeasurably.

Developing New Career Ladders

The biggest step forward for the nonprofessional movement, however, was the development of
new roles in the treatment scheme for the new
workers entering its ranks. While exciting
methods of training and satisfactory salaries did
give impetus to the paraprofessional program, it
was the revolutionary alterations in the treatment
"ladder" that provided the best long-range boost
for the movement.

Examples of administrations breaking up tasks
formerly performed by professionals alone, and
creating new responsible job functions for nonprofessionals, can be seen everywhere. In New York
City, prison workers (some of whom are ex-addicts
on methadone maintenance) function as screeners in

[4] National Institute of Labor Education, Mental Health
Program, The Indigenous Nonprofessional: A Strategy of
Change in Community Action and Community Health Programs,
New York, 1964.

a reception block. In Okinawa, Marine Corps
sergeants serve as group leaders and counselors—
positions formerly thought to be within the capabilities only of officers with college educations.
Paraprofessionals also are performing many tasks
traditionally done only by professional social
workers and parole officers.

CURRENT USE OF NONPROFESSIONALS
IN CORRECTIONS

Though the groundwork is still being laid for
many of the programs that will include paraprofessionals, much already has been accomplished in
projects involving nonspecialists. Among these
is the Providence Youth Interviewers Project,
where youths worked with their peers in individual
counseling and group sessions. The participants
reportedly gained both a sense of accomplishment
and an increased knowledge about themselves,
youth problems, and therapeutic programs. This
project also demonstrated that youths will con-
fide in their peers more readily than in adults,
when these peers are part of "the establishment."[5]

Much work has also been done with paraprofessionals in Danish prisons. In one experiment,
nonprofessionals were trained in principles of
group therapy. They were given advance experience
of the potential difficulties in leading a group—
for example, being criticized by equals, and
helping others in the group to take the lead—so
they could ultimately apply these talents on their
own, with only a minimum of senior staff supervision in follow-up sessions.[6] In another experiment, this time in the United States, a survey

[5]Progress for Providence, "Laying it on the line . . .
a report on the Providence Youth Interviewers Project,"
1966.

[6]Wulff Feldman, "Group counseling in Danish prisons,"
Police, 15 (1), 1970, pp. 40-44.

was done of two programs, the Riker's Island program of group counseling and the guided group interaction at Highfields. The investigator claimed that the use of nonprofessional leaders in each program seemed to change the character of the correctional institution. In fact, he felt that this innovation was a significant step in the transformation of the prison into a true correctional therapeutic community.[7]

Offenders as Manpower

Though the paraprofessional movement as a whole has injected new life into efforts to resocialize inmates, probably the most dynamic element of this approach is the inclusion of ex-offenders in the treatment scheme. In one program, a self-help therapeutic community was run entirely by ex-addicts, which appeared to lessen the reluctance of the inmates involved to relate to their treaters.[8] In another program, Project Re-Entry, the emphasis was slightly different. As Marie Buckley describes it,

> Project Re-Entry is a program through which ex-offenders who have "made it" on the outside voluntarily return to the prison on a regular basis. Their aim is to use their experience and insights to help men about to be released prepare themselves for a variety of problems they will meet on the outside.[9]

[7] Thomas A. Atlas, "An analytical survey of the use of group counseling in correctional institutions," Probation and Parole, No. 3, 1971, pp. 13-26.

[8] Robert M. Rapkin, "The NARA unit at Danbury: a short history of a unique treatment program for heroin addicts," American Journal of Correction, 33 (2), 1971, pp. 24-26.

[9] Marie Buckley, "Enter: the ex-con," Federal Probation, 36 (4), December, 1972, pp. 24-25.

Whatever the structure or philosophy of the approach that utilizes ex-offenders and offenders, it is foolish not to tap this resource. As Buckley points out, ". . . the successful released offender is an expert." J. D. Grant, in an article on the new careers development project, adds, "Evidence is now accumulating to the point where it can be considered a crime against the taxpayer not to develop strategies for the use of the offender as manpower in corrections and law enforcement programming." Since the staffing needs of corrections often parallel the occupational needs of offenders, using offenders for correctional manpower could be both therapeutically and financially sound.[10]

Nonprofessionals in Probation and Parole

The incredibly understaffed programs run by the departments of probation and parole seem to be ideal targets for the use of ex-offenders and other nonprofessionals. In the words of D. L. Loughery,

> Probation must get out of the country doctor era and into the age of the clinic. We can no longer waste the training of probation officers on inappropriate tasks. We are less in need of extra probation officers than we are in need of a corps of auxiliary workers to spread the effect of the officers we already have.[11]

[10] J. D. Grant, "The offender as a correctional manpower resource: new careers development project," in Frank Riessman and Hermine Popper (eds.), Up From Poverty: New Career Ladders for Nonprofessionals, Harper & Row, New York, 1968, p. 234.

[11] D. L. Loughery, Jr., "Innovations in probation management," Crime and Delinquency, 15 (2), 1969, pp. 247-258.

In some areas, these auxiliary workers might be volunteers from the community. In Japan, for example, most supervision of probations is carried out by volunteer probation officers. In the Kyoto prefecture alone there are a thousand volunteer officers. The probation officers themselves (in line with Loughery's suggestion) undertake very little casework and are mainly administrators of the volunteer force. [12]

Though the use of volunteers is widely considered to be an innovation, the concept is not at all new in corrections.

Probation in the United States was begun in 1841 by volunteers of whom John Augustus, a Boston cobbler, was the first. Today, over 200 courts in the United States, most of them adult misdemeanor or juvenile courts, are now using part- or full-time volunteers to provide correctional services. Many of these volunteers are well-educated, middle-class businessmen or professionals in other fields. . . .

Lee described the use of citizen volunteers from all walks of life in the circuit court juvenile department of Eugene, Oregon. They befriended youngsters with the implicit goal of enhancing performances in school, employment, family, and peer relationships. At present, the State of Oregon Division of Corrections is conducting an operation entitled "Project Most." Professional probation and parole officers have been involved in training nonprofessionals to work in teams with professionals. A few former offenders have been employed, and the staff reports a high degree of optimism about the impact the

[12] M. H. Hogan, "Probation in Japan," Probation, 17 (1), 1971, pp. 8-11.

nonprofessionals will have upon the Oregon correctional system. [13]

Students employed on a part-time and full-time basis have also achieved positive results in probation programs. In one summer project, 19 students from Anderson College in Indiana were given an opportunity to work in state probation offices. Sponsors of the project hoped that the probationers would be able to relate to the students more easily than to regular probation officers since the students were closer to their age. In addition, this experiment gave the students some experience with the criminal justice field, and a chance to see if it were an area they would like to enter for a career. The results of the project were encouraging. Students trained in criminal justice do seem to be able to help young probationers adjust successfully to society. The summer internships proved to be a good career-testing experience for the participants, and many judges and probation officers are eager to cooperate with such programs. [14]

Another study on paraprofessionals in probation was undertaken at the U.S. Probation and Parole Office in Chicago, Illinois. Sponsored by the University of Chicago's Center for Studies in Criminal Justice, this study examined the effects of part-time, indigenous paraprofessionals, some of whom were ex-offenders, on probation programs. The experiment's success was measured by the overall effects of the paraprofessionals' work on probationers, the amount of satisfaction they drew from their job, and the effect their participation in the program had on their career aspirations and attitudes. Although the findings of

[13] Donald W. Beless, William S. Pilcher, and Ellen Jo Ryan, "Use of indigenous nonprofessionals in probation and parole," Federal Probation, 1972, pp. 10-11.

[14] Val Clear, Summer Probation Internship Program 1971 (final report), Anderson College, Anderson, Indiana.

this study are still being evaluated, the experiment seems to have indicated that ". . . the paraprofessional position in corrections could serve as an entry point to a career line for Blacks and members of other minority groups with potential advancement to professional status contingent upon good performance, additional training, and achievement of an academic degree."[15]

NEW CAREER LINES

With the potential benefits of nonprofessionals to corrections established, it remains to discuss ways to make the best use of this source of manpower. This may be more difficult than it seems. To a large extent, corrections is still shrouded in a cloud of mystery, failure, destructive self-interest, apathy, and empire building. Providing new career lines for nonprofessionals is rather low on the priority list of many professionals.

Still, the problem is not insurmountable, and must be dealt with if the nonprofessional movement is to have any kind of direction. Accordingly, Benjamin, Freedman, and Lynton have noted two tentative career lines for nonprofessionals—one through casework, the other through group work. These two models set up three levels of advancement. Each successive level requires the worker to have more training and experience than the previous level, so he is adequately equipped to meet the greater responsibilities and challenges presented by each more advanced position. At the lowest level, the paraprofessional is screened and oriented. At the middle level he takes an active

[15] University of Chicago, Center for Studies in Criminal Justice, Second Progress Report (July 1, 1969-June 1, 1970) of the Probation Officer-Case Aide Project, by Donald W. Beless and William S. Pilcher, Chicago, 1970, p. 15.

role in casework or group work—for example, he
may make contacts in the community in an effort to
get an inmate a job. On a third level, the worker
operates under only limited supervision in a semi-
professional capacity. [16]

PROBLEMS AND LIMITATIONS

The expanding nonprofessional movement is
clearly a source for optimism in corrections.
However, several significant problems still limit
the extent and effectiveness of the use of paraprofessionals.

One of the most frustrating problems for
prison and mental health administrators is the
frequency with which nonprofessionals show up late
for their jobs, or not at all. Causes of this
unfortunate situation include the workers' low
salaries, the lack of structure in prison mental
health settings, the menial and boring duties
assigned to trainees in some agencies, and the
impatience of the nonprofessional to see his
efforts produce an impact on the system. Also,
many nonprofessionals simply do not share the
professionals' work ethic, and are indifferent to
the value and necessity of time schedules. Whatever the causes, though, paraprofessionals' tardi-
ness and excessive absences have stunted the
development of stable, valuable programs, and have
tarnished the early image of the movement.

Another problem looming over the programs
that employ paraprofessionals is the tendency of
project developers to ignore—intentionally or
unintentionally—the need to create new career
ladders. There is a great danger that

[16] Judith G. Benjamin, Marcia K. Freedman, and Edith F.
Lynton, "New careers in corrections," in Frank Riessman and
Hermine Popper (eds.), Up From Poverty: New Career Ladders
for Nonprofessionals, Harper & Row, 1968.

dollar-wise administrators will indiscriminately replace professionals with nonprofessionals just to save money. Or they may "ghettoize" the jobs nonprofessionals perform by assigning certain low-level jobs exclusively to untrained personnel who need work too badly to protest. Also, even some of the roles being developed specifically for the nonprofessional are dead end positions. Though they provide some training, have fair starting salaries, and can be satisfying for the new worker, they do not lead to any opportunities for advancement.

Some professionals also have reservations about the rationale underlying the whole paraprofessional movement. Ira Steisel mentioned several of these concerns in an article in Professional Psychology. One hope that he is dubious about is that nonprofessionals can communicate better with their patients because they have similar backgrounds. Steisel feels this natural rapport may be all but eliminated once the paraprofessional becomes attached to a formal structure. He also believes that the nonprofessional's capabilities may be more limited than advocates of the program would like to admit. Since nonprofessionals usually begin with only the barest acquaintance with psychological and medical techniques, they may not be able to give patients the help they need. In a situation where timing and decisive, informed action are often crucial, an untrained worker could do substantial harm. Moreover, considering that even psychiatrists often disagree about the causes of and best treatments for mental disorders, it is asking a great deal to expect a nonprofessional to detect and evaluate patients' problems.[17]

In spite of these and other serious problems that may limit the use of nonprofessionals, their

[17]Ira M. Steisel, "Paraprofessionals—questions from a traditionalist," Professional Psychology, 3 (3), 1972, pp. 331-334.

involvement in corrections still seems likely to
have a positive effect in many areas. For one
thing, the team approach, which makes use of all
available personnel resources including nonprofessionals and particularly ex-offenders, logically
should have more impact on patients than isolated
treatment by professionals alone. It is important
to remember that there is no one solution to
offender rehabilitation. The use of nonprofessionals is only part of the answer and should be
evaluated accordingly.

CORE REFERENCES

Beless, Donald, Pilcher, William, and Ryan,
Ellen Jo. "Use of indigenous nonprofessionals in
probation and parole," Federal Probation, March,
1972, pp. 10-15.
    A brief article on the use of nonprofessionals
in the area of probation and parole.

National Council on Crime and Delinquency.
Report of the [Professional Council] Subcommittee
on Study of the Use of Aides or Assistants in
Adult Probation Parole Agencies. Paramus, New
Jersey, 1971.
    A thorough discussion of the issues involved
in the use of paraprofessionals in probation and
parole.

Riessman, Frank, and Popper, Hermine (eds.).
Up from Poverty: New Career Ladders for Nonprofessionals. New York: Harper & Row, 1968.
    A collection of articles on the use of non-
professionals in varied fields.

Steisel, Ira. "Paraprofessionals—questions
from a traditionalist," Professional Psychology,
Vol. 3, No. 4, 1972, pp. 331-335.
    A good critique of the paraprofessional move-
ment in the mental health field.

Terwillinger, Carl. "The nonprofessional in correction," Crime and Delinquency, 12 (3), 1966, pp. 277-285.
A general article on the use of nonprofessionals in the correctional field.

CHAPTER 6

Prison
Violence

Tattered casualties of a prison riot may carry
indelible psychological scars away with them from
the scene of their nightmare. Unfortunately,
long after the molded weapons, buckshot, and tear
gas have been relegated to the harmless status of
litter, the memory of tearing flesh, blinding
fire, and sudden pervading panic remains. Interviews with correction officers held as hostages,
and rebellious confinees who were beaten into
surrendering, grimly bear this out. Thus, no one
is surprised to find administrators and researchers trying to find out what causes prison disturbances so they can prevent potential Atticas
in their own systems.

PRISON RIOTS

Riots once were accepted as inevitable in
the prison setting. Many people expected
"society's lost, violent members" to be incapable
of controlling their animal-like impulses. After
all, isn't that why they were sent to jail in the
first place?

Today, however, behavioral scientists
strongly reject such a simplistic, biased view.

Prison Violence

The presence of aggressive, antisocial offenders
in prisons is obviously a contributing factor, but
the specific cause of a single disturbance or riot
is now understood to include numerous institutional and noninstitutional precipitating and pre-
disposing elements. Most prison disturbances can
be traced to one or more of the following problems: public ignorance, apathy, or hostility
toward rehabilitative efforts; inadequate personnel; limited facilities; lack of effective work
and therapy programs; certain offenders' personalities; poor communications; and judicial
inequities.

Public Attitude

Community interest in correctional treatment—or more accurately, the usual lack of
interest—is one of the major causes of institutional disturbances. When citizens do express
concern over the actions of prison administrators
and correctional psychologists, it is often
because they feel these officials are too lenient.
This punitive attitude is responsible for the type
of penal institutions most common at present:
Though only approximately one-third of the
offenders now institutionalized need to be kept
under maximum security, 80 to 90 percent of the
total inmate population is still housed in
"archaic forts."[1]

Even more serious than such punitiveness is
society's general apathy about what is going on
behind prison walls and in community-based
correction settings. This indifference is
reflected by the legislators who control the
purse strings of the nation's budget. Although
more funds are now being allocated to corrections,
few people appreciate how much money is really
needed, and how much of it is wasted when
"rehabilitation" consists only of locking up an
inmate in an overcrowded, factory-like structure.

[1]Frank T. Flynn, "Behind prison riots," Social Service
Review, vol. 27, 1953, p. 77.

The result of this public attitude is expressed
by Christian Century:

> The riots result, we believe, not from bad
> prison conditions or practices but from the
> belief of prison inmates that the only way
> in which they can gain public interest in
> improving such conditions is by rioting.
> Nonviolent protests or requests for remedial
> action, prisoners believe, never accomplish
> anything. Riots sometimes do.[2]

Unfortunately, many citizens evidently prefer
not to be concerned with inmate treatment. They
almost seem to believe that if they don't think
about crimes, or the people who commit them, the
crime problem will go away. Those who do devote
some thought to how offenders should be treated
often are divided between a rational and an
emotional attitude. While they realize intellectually that punishment is of little value and that
society is responsible for effective rehabilitation, they still crave retribution when a crime
is committed. Thus, while stacks of material
have been written on humane correctional methods,
only a small proportion of the suggestions made
has ever been implemented.

Inadequate Personnel and Limited Facilities

Few penal institutions can boast a staff that
is adequate in both size and quality. The poor
salaries and limited facilities that have
resulted from lack of funds have discouraged many
qualified persons from entering the correctional
field. Most correction officers are substantially underpaid, and in many penal systems
psychologists as well receive inadequate
salaries. This is especially unfortunate because,
as the National Task Force on Corrections states,

---

[2] "What do the prison riots signify?" Christian Century,
vol. 72, p. 884.

> To obtain competent people with the required
> aptitudes . . . requires financial induce-
> ment beyond the prevailing salary rate.
> Such an amount might, for example, be fixed
> at 20% above the prevailing regional rate
> for an occupation.[3]

Naturally, correcting the personnel shortage
is still only a partial answer. Effective treatment also requires an adequate physical plant
that is not overcrowded, outmoded, or without
areas where rehabilitative programs can be conducted. The penitentiary in Ohio that was rocked
by a riot in 1968 was 102 years old at the time,
and when disturbances erupted at the Manhattan
House of Detention in New York City in August of
1970, that facility was operating at 220 percent
of capacity. Although a new facility does not
automatically eliminate riots (Utah State Prison
had a riot when it was only six years old), it
does seem to increase the odds against one
occurring.

Lack of Meaningful Work and Programs

Inmate idleness is another factor that contributes to the development of riot conditions.
Some of the obstacles that prevent prisons from
providing good work programs for prisoners
include pressure from local industry and labor
unions who fear economic competition from the
inmates; insufficient "chasers" (C.O. escorts) to
supervise and guard inmates while they work;
prisoners' lack of training; and the large number
of unsentenced prisoners, who cannot be assigned
to jobs.

---

[3]Task Force on Corrections of the President's Commis-
sion on Law Enforcement and Administration of Justice,
Task Force Report: Corrections, U.S. Government Printing
Office, Washington, D.C., 1967, pp. 94-95.

Particularly in urban areas, local industry and labor unions sometimes oppose prison work programs because they fear competition from inmates. Some correctional administrators dealt with this problem by developing projects that will not compete with local firms. Setting up trade unions for qualified inmates should further alleviate this problem, and also help ensure that the offender will get a decent position when he is released.

Another cause of idleness, particularly in military confinement centers, has been the lack of sufficient "chasers" to escort and supervise working inmates. In one prison, the Camp Butler Correctional Facility in Okinawa, officials solved this problem by training members of the unit for whom the military prisoners were going to work.

Probably the most serious cause of inmate idleness, however, is the overwhelming number of unsentenced prisoners in detention. Since prisoners who have not yet been sentenced are supposed to be housed without being punished, they cannot be forced to work or to remain working. If they work at all, it is as a free alternative to doing nothing. Thus, the activities they are asked to volunteer for must be interesting and challenging. Unfortunately, most institutions are not geared to offer such work.

Offender Personalities

Hans Toch divided inmates prone to violence into two classes. Within these classes are two main types: those who act violently as a means of raising their worth in their own opinion and that of their peers, and self-centered individuals who see others as objects to be manipulated as the need arises. In the first category are reputation defenders, norm enforcers, self-image defenders, and pressure removers. The second category includes bullies, exploiters, self-indulgent personalities, and people who use violence as a catharsis.[4]

Earl Ward, convicted of robbery, polygamy, and falsely claiming to have committed homicide, is an example of the offender who exhibits pronounced antisocial tendencies during confinement. While in Michigan Prison, Ward took decisive parts in two disturbances. The first incident was an attempt to escape, involving a plot to kidnap the governor. In the second riot Ward coordinated (successful) efforts to force the governor to accept a list of terms presented by the inmates as a condition to halting the disturbance. During this second riot, Ward marshalled and led a large body of disorganized prisoners, held negotiations and press conferences, and directed the head-quarters set up in his cell, where he also held hostages.

When questioned later, Ward noted that he was proud of his cool-headed leadership. He showed no remorse for his actions and admitted that he would have given the word to cut the throats of the hostages if state troopers had tried to defy his authority.[5] Ward's actions during the riot and his reactions afterwards illustrate how very dangerous antisocial prisoners can be. It is not surprising that disturbances often start in the section of a prison where most of these prisoners are housed, and where they have had time to organize.

However, manipulative inmates prone to violence are still only one potential cause of prison disturbances. If the presence of such

[4] Hans Toch, Violent Men, Aldine, Chicago, 1969, pp. 135-136.

[5] G. M. Gilbert, Personality Dynamics: A Biosocial Approach, Harper & Row, New York, 1970, pp. 318-322. Donald R. Cressey (ed.), The Prison: Studies in Institutional Organization and Change, Holt, Rinehart & Winston, New York, 1961, p. 265.

offenders guaranteed a riot, hardly an institution anywhere could operate without one.

Poor Communication and Judicial Inequities

Of the other factors leading to riotous conditions, two of the most prominent are poor communications and judicial inequities. Their detrimental effect on inmate morale has been a problem for a long time. Communications among staff members are usually poor enough, but as Goffman points out, the situation is even worse between staff and inmates.

> Each group tends to conceive of the other in terms of narrow, hostile stereotypes: Staff often see inmates as bitter, secretive and untrustworthy, while inmates often see staff as condescending, highhanded, and mean.[6]

If effective formal and informal lines of communication were open between staff and inmates, prejudice and unfair stereotyping might be lessened. However, most facilities have either inadequate informal channels open to confinees, or a cumbersome, rigid formal line that is not responsive to inmates' immediate needs.

Overwhelmed by a strange, threatening institutional environment, a first offender who does not speak English often has many problems which become magnified when he cannot communicate them to others. If an inmate is not told how to arrange to see a relative, social worker, psychologist, or chaplain soon after being incarcerated, he may become frightened and upset enough to self-mutilate. Yet, many correctional facilities today make it almost impossible for an inmate to relate his feelings to someone until he has been in the facility for a dangerously long time.

[6]Erving Goffman, "On the characteristics of total institutions: the inmate world," in Cressey (ed.), ibid., p. 18.

Judicial inequities by parole boards, the courts, and prison infraction boards also incense inmates. The inconsistency of punishment convinces the disadvantaged offender that "justice" is a wealthy man's toy. While one man is released on $100,000 bail, another sits in his cell for nine months awaiting trial because he can't raise $500. As one first offender is convicted of theft and sentenced to five years, the gavel can send another person convicted of the same crime to six months. About judicial inequities one can safely say they are widespread and shameful.

RIOT PREVENTION AND THE BEHAVIORAL SCIENTIST

The correctional psychologist, his fellow behavioral scientists, and mental health personnel have a special role in preventing penal disturbances. Like all correctional workers, they are expected to review reports and studies on causes of disturbances. Beyond this function, though, those trained in correctional psychology and psychiatry have an even more unique service to offer. Because of their ability to pinpoint and understand the problems that arise when individuals and groups interact—or fail to interact— in an institutional setting, mental health personnel are being called in more and more to examine, consult, and recommend changes or procedures to prevent potential disturbances. Riots bring bad publicity and pressure to bear on correctional administrators. On the other hand, traditional methods of suppressing prisoners who seem likely to riot are often not effective and are, for the most part, no longer tolerated by society. Accordingly, for political as well as humanitarian reasons, the behavioral scientists (including those in the psychiatric and social work professions) are at last being allowed to become involved in riot prevention programs. This involvement should lead to a better understanding of why disturbances occur in our prison systems, and the resulting knowledge can be applied in the future to prevent such tragedies from happening again.

Ideally, those in the behavioral professions will also be in a position to initiate policies and actions that could prevent riotous conditions from developing. These might include instructing and encouraging correctional personnel to be sensitive to problem areas and early signs of tension, such as increased self-segregation by ethnic or racial groups; emphasizing the need for all staff to take prompt action on inmates' legitimate grievances; aiding in the identification and treatment of aggressive antisocial inmates; increasing the flow of information to inmates on issues affecting their welfare; and ensuring that the programs provided for offenders are productive, not just busy-work.

SELF-MUTILATION AND SUICIDE

That people express concern when they hear of a case of self-mutilation or suicide is no surprise. Self-injurious behavior is baffling and tragic, and often points to the presence of unrecognized intolerable situations. But with all the attention that self-mutilation generally elicits, little real information about prison suicides and self-injurious behavior has been available to the public. As Thomas O'Rourke points out,

> Scant research has been published in the areas of suicide, attempted suicide and self-mutilation by prison inmates. Fear of bad public review and the general inaccessibility of the correctional systems of most states have often condemned professionals to ignorance about the problems with which

97

they must deal, at the same time denying them enlightened methods of treatment.[7]

This is particularly unfortunate since, as Wolfram Rieger notes, "The 'closed society' of a prison where even the slightest suicidal gesture is officially recorded lends itself ideally to a study of suicide attempts."[8] Furthermore, this lack of information on prison self-mutilation becomes an even more serious issue when one sees that self-mutilation and suicide represent a significant problem in many penal systems. In 1970, the New York City prisons, which had 100,000 admissions, had 10 inmates successfully commit suicide, and scores injured themselves.[9]

Consequently, correctional psychologists and administrators have had to rely on only a few thorough studies while waiting for reports on the promising investigations now being conducted by such researchers as Toch, O'Rourke, Gibbs, and Danto. From the studies currently available—many of which are unpublished manuscripts—several tentative points have come to light regarding the causes, treatment, and prevention of self-mutilation and suicide in prisons.

Causes

In many instances, self-injurious behavior (SIB) and suicide attempts seem to occur more frequently during one phase of confinement than

[7]Thomas O'Rourke, "A descriptive study of suicide, attempted suicide and self-mutilation in New York City Prisons," unpublished, New York, 1972, p. 1.

[8]Wolfram Rieger, "Suicide attempts in a federal prison," Archives of General Psychiatry, June, 1971, vol. 24, p. 532.

[9]D. Cooper and M. Baden, "Suicide in prison: report to the health research training program of the New York City Department of Health, 1971."

another. For example, according to Stengel, the risk of suicide is high among inmates in the early part of imprisonment.[10] As one might expect, the chance of SIB is also greater when an inmate is under stress or in a state of depression. The frustration or depression produced by the initial shock of being incarcerated, coupled with the expectation of being sentenced to remain isolated and powerless in prison for a long or undefined period, leads to aggression and hostility that is often directed inward.

The causes of stress or depression great enough to prompt a confinee to injure himself are numerous. In an article dealing with suicide among marcotic addicts, Michael Baden says, "The disgrace of arrest, feelings of hopelessness, and drug withdrawal in a basically suicidal individual may encourage suicide attempts."[11] Some precipitating causes also relate to the offender's institutionalization in an abnormal environment (most prisons qualify for such a label). Beto and Claghorn mention "fear of homosexual attack; death in the family and his inability to be there; fear of brutality from other inmates or guards; or a 'dear John' letter from his wife or girl friend" as some of these causes.[12] To them we can add receiving an "unexpected sentence of unusually long duration handed down by the courts; guilt arising from a crime committed by the individual which had particularly unpleasant overtones (child molesting, murder of a relative or close friend)

[10] E. Stengel, "Suicide in prison: the gesture and the risk," Prison Service Journal, Manchester, England, vol. 2, 1971, pp. 13-14.

[11] Michael M. Baden, "Homicide, suicide, and accidental death among narcotic addicts," Human Pathology, vol. 3, No. 1, March 1972, p. 94.

[12] Dan Richard Beto and James L. Claghorn, "Factors associated with self-mutilation within the Texas department of corrections," American Journal of Correction, Jan.-Feb., 1968, p. 25.

Prison Violence

. . . (and) confinement for a long period in an
unsentenced status."[13]

The prison social structure also contributes
to the problem of self-mutilation. This is made
clear in a study by Johnson and Britt, one of the
most extensive works done on self-mutilation in
prisons to date. The authors noted four major
ways the prison social structure worsens the
problem of SIB: (1) It is deficient in providing outlets for tension for inmates who have
demonstrated an inability to deal with tension
in effective and socially acceptable ways; (2)
Under certain circumstances, self-mutilation is
considered a "normal" attempt to adjust to the
prison environment; (3) Self-mutilation can
qualify the inmate for the "sick" role, thereby
winning him a transfer from close custody; and
(4) The prison administration's main objective
is running a "quiet joint," so inmates are
encouraged to suppress rather than express their
problems.[14]

Generally, then, prisoner self-mutilation
could probably be attributed to one or more of
the goals listed on the following page.

Self-Mutilator and Suicidal Inmate

In attempting to recognize the causes for
self-mutilation, researchers have naturally also
tried to identify the type of offender who is
statistically prone to opt for SIB as a solution
to his problems. Tuckman and Youngman, looking
for a possible relationship between suicide and
past history of recorded criminal behavior, found
no significant difference between 172 suicides
and a matched control group of 148 persons who

[13]Robert J. Wicks, "Suicide prevention: a brief for corrections officers," Federal Probation, Sept., 1972, p. 30.

[14]Elmer Johnson and Benjamin Britt, Self-Mutilation
in Prison: Interaction of Stress and Social Structure,
Center for the Study of Crime, Delinquency and Corrections,
Southern Illinois University, 1967.

100

GOALS OF THE PRISON SELF-MUTILATOR

1. ## Reclassification

   a. Inmate believes a suicidal gesture will get him transferred to isolation, where he will be safe from the rest of the population and will be treated more humanely.

   b. Offender wants to demonstrate his ability to control his own destiny, by forcing the prison administration to reclassify him.

   c. Prisoner wants to be transferred out of segregation and to be united with other inmates in the dorm.

2. ## Cry for Help

   a. General attention-getting device after other channels have proved too slow or frustrating.

   b. Need for services (drugs, better food, medical treatment, psychiatric help).

   c. Help in dealing with institutional staff, who have ignored or aggravated his problems.

3. ## Escape from Intolerable Situations

   a. Desire to avoid the continued realization that he has committed a terrible crime or has led a miserably wasted existence (especially drug addicts).

   b. Escape from prison environment.

   c. Escape from depression caused by bad news, no news, homosexual rape, or other precipitating event.

4. ## Desire for Clemency

   a. To have it noted on his record that he attempted suicide, so that the judge will have cause to be lenient with him.

   b. As a method to convince staff and peers that they should be good to him, since he is obviously in need of special treatment.

died from natural causes.[15] Beto and Claghorn, on
the other hand, did report significant differences
between 50 self-mutilators and a control group on
a number of other variables. In a study at the
Wynne Treatment Center, data were gathered through
questionnaires and personal interviews. Six
factors were found to be significant; the most
important of these was race.

> The Negroes, who make up 36.35% of the total
> prison population, contributed only 6% (3)
> of the mutilators. On the other hand, the
> Latin Americans who make up 17.74% of the
> prison population, have a total of 36% (18)
> of the mutilators.[16]

Although these findings point to a higher
instance of self-mutilation among Latin Americans
than among blacks, O'Rourke aptly notes that "a
question remains as to whether this is due to a
racial characteristic, regional differences or
even a bias in administrative response prejudicing
sample selection."[17] Moreover, the size of their
sample was too small to justify any firm conclusions.

Johnson and Britt's study of SIB indicated
that self-mutilators could be divided into four
categories: emotionally unstable, passive-
aggressive, impulsive psychopathic, and antisocial.
They found that self-mutilators came from backgrounds that were deficient in family stability,
educational attainment, and mental normality.
Self-mutilators also showed a higher incidence

[15] J. Tuckman and W. F. Youngman, "Suicide and criminality," Journal of Forensic Science, vol. 10, 1965, pp. 104-
107.

[16] Beto and Claghorn, op. cit., pp. 25-27.

[17] O'Rourke, op. cit., p. 4.

of previous hospitalization for mental problems than other inmates.[18]

Britt also reported that in comparison to the general prison population, the self-mutilator was younger, predominately white, a recidivist, in prison for a more aggressive crime and for a longer sentence, more often single, less intelligent, untrained occupationally, and had an overall history of failures. In addition, he often showed a history of drug addiction or alcoholism, or had chronic psychological difficulties and problems coping with life both in prisons and in society.[19]

Preventive Measures

Besides sketching a description of the self-mutilator and noting some of the pronounced causes of suicidal behavior, studies done in this area have also made recommendations on how SIB can be prevented. One of the points most often emphasized is that the correction officer (C.O.) should be trained to assist in suicide prevention. Bruce Danto avers that the guard or deputy will have his rescue role accepted by inmates if he learns to accept his limitations, comes to terms with his own feelings about death, and presents himself to the inmates as a real person rather than a "bleeding heart do-gooder."[20] Also, if the C.O. is to be effective, he must be adequately trained. Prison officials share most of the misconceptions about suicide that are held by the general public. And since it is the C.O., not the psychologist, who is usually on the spot when an offender attempts suicide or SIB, it is unfair to him as well as to

[18]Johnson and Britt, op. cit.

[19]Benjamin E. Britt, "Self-mutilation and dynamics of imprisonment," unpublished, Raleigh, N.C., 1967.

[20]Bruce L. Danto, "The suicidal inmate," Police Chief, vol. 38 (8), 1971, pp. 56-59.

his charges to expect him to deal with such an emotionally charged situation unless he has been trained to do so.

Two of the recommendations of the New York City Board of Correction for maximizing use of the C.O. are sensitivity training for C.O.'s who have direct and frequent contact with the prisoners, and the development of a system to ensure that information on disturbed inmates is passed on from shift to shift. The Board's other recommendations for cutting down suicide and SIB, though not dealing directly with the line officer, are as follows:

1. Plans for more psychiatric and medical wards, including more dormitory-style prison facilities, should be developed.

2. The custodians who deliver prisoners from the courts to an institution should report any disturbing prisoner behavior they observe so that the receiving officers can make appropriate classification assignments.

3. A program of orientation for prisoners should be organized so that new inmates will understand prison discipline and expectations, and so that prisoners will have an opportunity to ask questions regarding their care.

4. More Spanish-speaking personnel must be employed at all levels of the department.

5. The administration should assist Hispanic prisoners in adjusting by (a) developing programs to teach them English, (b) providing more books in Spanish for prison libraries, (c) employing bilingual detainees as interpreters for Spanish-speaking inmates (one inmate, to be available around the clock, should be designated in each housing area to communicate with non-English-speaking inmates), and (d) by permitting the celebration of Hispanic cultural events in prison.

6. Inmate classification programs must be set up.

7. Inmates who have already experienced similar difficulties with prison life might be valuable as observers or helpers for newer inmates.[21]

From these recommendations, it seems evident that the methods generally employed to prevent suicide and reduce self-mutilation fall into two broad categories: developing a team approach to deal with the problem, and eliminating precipi-tating institutional factors. The team approach to both crisis intervention and long-range prevention of SIB should emphasize the use and training of the C.O., sensitive inmates, mental health personnel, and arresting and court officers. Their training should include minority group awareness sessions, sensitivity groups, and creative programs on symptomatology and human relations techniques. In addition to developing these full-time teams, administration and psychologists must examine their facility's weak spots and make the changes needed to ensure that the prison environment does not undo the efforts of its staff.

Recognition of a problem does not usually result in automatic corrective action in either penal facilities or the overall criminal justice system. Mountains of private studies have been done on crises and tragedies in corrections, as well as the need for judicial and parole reform, but they have not led to action because they were initiated only to salve public outrage and avert public pressure. Unless this trend to act only on paper changes for the better, no matter how thoroughly the behavioral scientist researches

[21] New York City Board of Correction, "Report on prison suicides and urgent recommendations for action," New York, 1972.

105

and plans, desperate men will continue to do
desperate things to solve their dilemmas, and
violent behavior in prisons will increase, not
decrease.

CORE REFERENCES

Prison Riots and Disturbances

American Correctional Association. Riots &
Disturbances. Washington, D.C.: American Correctional Association, 1970.
    A fine, contemporary treatment of the causes,
prevention, and handling of prison disturbances.

Self-Mutilation and Suicide
in the Penal Setting

Johnson, Elmer, and Britt, Benjamin. Self-
Mutilation in Prison: Interaction of Stress and
Social Structure. Carbondale, Ill.: Center for
the Study of Crime, Delinquency and Corrections,
Southern Illinois University, 1967.
    A thorough study of inmate self-mutilation.

Danto, Bruce L. (ed.). Jail House Blues
Orchard Lake, Michigan: Epic, 1973.
    This recently published collection of articles
on suicide in the correctional setting contains
essential information for anyone interested in
this area.

CHAPTER 7

Unusual Problems
in Corrections

A prison is a strange and often abnormally
destructive environment for a human being. To
adjust to it, staff and inmates alike need to
muster all of their personal resources. However,
when a penal environment's unique stresses out-
weigh an individual's ability to cope with them,
unusual problems may result. Two particular
difficulties of this type the correctional
psychologist often encounters involve the areas
of prison sexuality and the working relationship
between treatment and custodial staffs.

PRISON SEXUALITY

Sexual assaults and rampant homosexuality
continue to be part of the daily scene in most of
our prisons today. A three-month study conducted
by the Philadelphia District Attorney's office and
Police Department found that sexual assaults in
the Philadelphia Prison System were of "epidemic"
proportions. During a 26-month period, 156 sexual
assaults were documented and substantiated in the
system. These assaults involved at least 97
different victims and at least 176 different
aggressors. From their data and observations, the
investigators estimated that about 2,000 sex

assaults had occurred during the period of the
study, and only 64 were mentioned in prison
records. Of the 64, 40 resulted in disciplinary
action against the aggressors; 26 were reported
to the police for prosecution.[1]

The impact of a homosexual attack in prison,
or the threat of it, can be quite traumatic, as
can be seen in a report by G. B. Smith, a psychiatric consultant:

> Many of our patients in the Psychiatric
> Division are young. Twenty-seven are under
> the age of twenty, one hundred ninety-seven
> under thirty. Many of these youthful
> patients have been transferred to our
> psychiatric facility from Pontiac (where
> Illinois segregates its youthful first
> offenders) due to a schizophrenic reaction
> following a homosexual panic.[2]

Size of the Problem

Anyone familiar with a prison environment
today is aware that homosexuality is an overwhelming problem. Yet, one basic question still
remains unanswered: How frequently does homosexual behavior in prison actually occur? As one
investigator of sex deviation in the prison community notes, "We cannot tell how frequent because
we lack reliable statistics. It is, we think, so
frequent that we may call it an 'occupational
hazard' to being an inmate."[3]

[1]Alan J. Davis, "Sexual assaults in the Philadelphia
prison system and sheriff's vans," Trans-action, 6 (2),
1968, pp. 8-16.

[2]Arthur V. Huffman, "Problems precipitated by homosexual
approaches," Journal of Social Therapy, vol. 7, 1961,
p. 221.

[3]Arthur V. Huffman, "Sex deviation in a prison community," Journal of Social Therapy, vol. 6, 1960, p. 180.

The rate of homosexuality appears to be so high in urban female institutions that Bluestone, O'Malley, and Connell were prompted to state that "In institutions for female offenders, a homosexual orientation is so common that no attempt can be made to separate these individuals from the seemingly heterosexual group. . . . In our experience, a remarkably high percentage of offenders sentenced to this institution—we estimate this to be as high as 80 to 90% of the inmates we have seen—have a definite history of homosexuality."[4]

However, these figures must be viewed as exactly what they are—estimates. An accurate picture of the incidence of prison homosexuality has always been difficult to obtain for a number of reasons. Inmates are reluctant to be open about their homosexual encounters because they fear that prison authorities may remove them to another housing area or deny them parole, or because they want to forget such involvement when they are close to release back into a heterosexually oriented society. Staff, too, for any number of varied motivations may repress studies in this area. Accordingly, the validity and reliability of existing estimates of homosexual behavior in penal settings are open to some doubt. Buffum notes that some of the variance between different estimates also results from "the intensity of institutional custody, the social origin of the prison population, and the duration of the individual sentence."[5] All these factors are reflected in the estimates in Table 1.

[4]Harvey Bluestone, Edward P. O'Malley, and Sydney Connell, "Homosexuals in prison," Corrective Psychiatry and Journal of Social Therapy, vol. 12, no. 1, 1966, p. 15.

[5]Peter C. Buffum, Homosexuality in Prisons, U.S. Dept. of Justice, LEAA, National Institute of Law Enforcement and Criminal Justice, 1972, p. 13.

Table 1

Investigator	Estimated Proportion of Inmate Population Who Have Had Homosexual Experiences
Clemmer[a]	40%
Sykes [b]	35%
Fishman[c]	30-40%
Thomas[d]	80-90%
Irwin[e]	7%

[a]Donald Clemmer, "Some aspects of sexual behavior in the prison community," Proceedings of the American Correctional Association, 1958.

[b]Gresham Sykes, The Society of Captives, Princeton University Press, Princeton, New Jersey, 1958.

[c]Joseph Fishman, Sex in Prison, National Library Press, New York, 1934.

[d]Herbert E. Thomas, "Regressive maladaptive behavior in maximum security prisoners," revised working paper for the conference on prison homosexuality, Oct. 14-15, 1971, p. 9.

[e]John Irwin, "Some research questions on homosexuality in jails and prisons," revised working paper for the conference on prison homosexuality, Oct. 14-15, 1971.

Homosexual Influences in Prison

It is an accepted fact that prison life contributes to an increase in the incidence of homosexual behavior. What is still in question is the amount of influence it has and the way in which it furthers homosexuality. According to Bluestone, O'Malley, and Connell, "prisons do not contribute to the onset of homosexuality any more than do socially approved single-sex institutions such as boarding schools and military institutions.

. . . The simple fact is that there is a greater percentage of homosexuals in prisons than in the general population, particularly in institutions for sentenced females. Prisons are not selective but must admit all those sent from court."[6]

Benjamin Karpman, in The Sexual Offender and His Offenses, particularly emphasizes the crowded, single-sex environment in prisons as being a significant encouragement for homosexual behavior.

Much of the external physical environment in prison favors the development of sexual abnormalities. Cells are often overcrowded, three and more may be in one cell. . . . As often as not, a young delinquent may be put in the same cell with a much older offender and it is not long before the former has to give in, or else, not infrequently, risk his life. The situation is even more diffi- cult and trying when prisoners are put to sleep in dormitories instead of cells. Beds are put very close and the sight and smell of naked bodies, the parading and exposure which is unavoidable, charge the atmosphere with excessive stimulation. Aside from all this, time plays heavily on the prisoner. Even if he is fully occupied with work during the day—and many prisons fall short of such provision—he is still left with a great deal of time to himself. In the conversations exchanged, the favorite topics, because practically the only topics left, are crime and sex, sex and crime. When alone, there is readier phantasy indulgence, compensating for unpleasant reality, and this not only provides the matrix for masturbation and homosexual phantasy indulgence, but equally incapaci- tates the individual for life on the outside when he is discharged.[7]

[6]Bluestone et al., op. cit., pp. 20-21.

[7]Benjamin Karpman, in "Problems precipitated by homo- sexual approaches in youthful first offenders," by Arthur Huffman, Journal of Social Therapy, vol. 7, 1961, pp. 216- 217.

As one might expect, other elements also
contribute to homosexual behavior in the prison
setting. Some of these other factors are cited
by Arthur Huffman in his presentation of one
inmate's observations on homosexuality in prison.
Three of the confinee's observations were: (1) a
juvenile recidivist who has had previous homosexual experiences and contacts in other institutions is likely to do the same in his new confinement facility; (2) the prison "caste system" and
"grapevine" announces its expectations regarding
a prisoner's sex role and holds him to it; and
(3) "commercial homosexuals" who sell themselves
for favors encourage the practice of homosexuality
in a prison.[8]

In the case of the woman offender, some of the
factors that increase homosexuality seem to be
different. Max Hammer, for example, indicates
that some female offenders consider femininity to
mean dependency and passivity, which they view
negatively.

Masculinity is seen by these women as something positive and they equate masculinity
with such terms as autonomy, aggressiveness,
potency and freedom from restrictions.
Femininity is not seen as anything positive
but rather the absence of something positive,
therefore they feel that to be feminine is
to be castrated, vulnerable, restricted, etc.[9]

Sex and Prison Homosexuality

As Hammer's statement indicates, the gender of
the inmate seems to affect the shape of inmate
sexuality. In the case of the male, a homosexual

[8]Arthur Huffman, "Sex deviation in a prison community,"
Journal of Social Therapy, vol. 6, 1960, p. 172.

[9]Max Hammer, "Homosexuality in a women's reformatory,"
Corrective Psychiatry and Journal of Social Therapy,
vol. 11, no. 3, pp. 168-169.

experience frequently occurs when an inmate needs
an outlet for physical urges, or wants to reinforce his masculinity by being the aggressive
partner in a homosexual act. Such motivations
are only minor for females.

> The typical response of women to the
> depersonalizing and alienating environment
> of the penal institution differs substan-
> tially from that of the males. Nearly
> universally in juvenile institutions, and
> in some observed cases in institutions for
> adult females, female prisoners appear to
> form into pseudo-families with articulated
> roles. . . . A minor part of overt female
> homosexual contacts may arise from depriva-
> tion of sexuality, but the primary source
> is the deprivation of emotionally satisfy-
> ing relationships with members of the
> opposite sex and the desire to create the
> basis for a community of relationships that
> are stable and predictable. . . . The homo-
> sexual relationship offers protection from
> the exigencies of the environment and the
> physical homosexual contacts are less
> sought for physical release that they afford
> than for the validation of emotionally bind-
> ing and significant relationships.[10]

Differences between a female offender's homosexual relationship and a male's are especially
evident from the data on inmate self-mutilation.
In male institutions, offenders have been known
to attempt suicide following a homosexual act.
In female facilities, on the other hand, lesbian
activities often appear to lessen the tendency
for an inmate to self-mutilate. One of the main
reasons for this contrast appears to be the
meaningful emotional outlets, close relationships, and pseudo-family structures that female
homosexual pairs and groups form.

---

[10] Buffum, op. cit., p. 21.

Defining the Problem

From the results of these studies on prison
sexuality and reports on the problem of institutional homosexuality, a number of general points
can tentatively be made (see the list on the following page). And upon reviewing them, one rather surprising factor comes to light. The overt street homosexual does not seem to be the core of the problem for prison authorities. This hypothesis is supported by Huffman:

> It is perhaps an ironic paradox that the
> true homosexual plays but little part in the
> surging tide of sexuality that ebbs and flows
> within the walls of a large prison. In point
> of numbers, the true homosexual is a rara avis
> since his effeminate secondary characteristics
> are so obvious that he is always closely
> watched by the guards and other officials.
> Consequently these lifelong homosexuals, who
> are almost entirely fellators, find that their
> sexual proclivities are so restricted by
> constant watchfulness that they have but
> little opportunity to engage in the perver-
> sion of their choosing and, while they may
> serve a fairly large number of the inmates
> with outlets on the rare occasions that they
> are out from under surveillance, their impact
> on the homosexual force of the institution
> as a whole is relatively minor. [11]

The problem of prison homosexuality instead
seems to lie mainly with the aggressive sociopaths, commercial homosexuals, and juvenile
recidivists who have had former institutional
homosexual experiences. It is on these groups
that the psychologist and correctional administrator must concentrate.

Dealing with the Problem

A major obstacle to effective intervention in
the problem of prison homosexuality is many
administrators' and psychologists' pessimism about

[11] Huffman, op. cit., pp. 172-173.

HOMOSEXUALITY IN PRISON

1. Sexual assaults and homosexuality exist in penal settings to an unacceptable degree, but the extent of the problem is not reflected currently by definitely reliable figures.

2. Female correctional facilities seem to have a greater incidence of homosexuality.

3. In general, female offenders view homosexuality differently from their male counterparts.

4. Many offenders have had homosexual experiences prior to incarceration.

5. Institutional factors encouraging homosexual behavior include:

   a. Single-sex environment.

   b. Close, overcrowded housing areas.

   c. Lack of meaningful work and recreation.

   d. Demands of "prison caste system" for inmate to fill a certain sex role.

   e. Absence of opportunities for physical release of sex drive.

   f. Need for offender to demonstrate masculine role and to show himself to be independent and dominant not fulfilled in prison.

   g. Lack of opportunity to form meaningful social relationships.

the effectiveness of any method slated to deal
with it. One of the current assumptions is "Even
the best wardens in the best prisons cannot cope
with this problem. It cannot be eliminated in
such unwholesome surroundings." [12]

Yet, prison homosexuality must be dealt with
today. Young and impressionable inmates may
become confused about their sex role after long
confinement in a single-sex institution. Being
confronted with seduction and homosexuality can
only make their situation worse. Add to this the
problems raised by physically forced homosexuality
and "homosexual love triangles" in the penal
setting, and the need for action becomes evident.
Furthermore, as Vernon Fox notes, "In some jails,
too, ruthless and aggressive prisoners extort
money and other things from weaker prisoners.
Much homosexual behavior begins in this manner." [13]

Some of the types of intervention open to
those in penal work are isolation, group or
individual therapy, redirection of sexual drives,
legal action, conjugal and home visits, chemo-
therapy (hormone treatment—rarely used), and
operative treatment. This last alternative,
although still much disputed, has been employed
in Denmark since 1929 when a law was passed making
it possible for sex offenders to consent to castra-
tion. It is necessary for the offender himself to
apply for it on the grounds that his sexual urge
causes him to commit crimes rendering him harmful
to society.

Identification and isolation of the inmate
homosexual and rapist is the traditional method
of treating prison sexuality problems. This
approach is employed in an effort to reduce the

[12] Clyde Vedder and Patricia King, Problems of Homosexuality in Corrections, Charles C. Thomas, Springfield, 1971,
p. 40.

[13] Vernon Fox, Introduction to Corrections, Prentice-
Hall, Englewood Cliffs, N.J., 1972, p. 89.

probability that one inmate rapist will come into
violent conflict with another for the favors of
other homosexuals, to lessen the chance for more
than one rapist to gang up on a weak inmate, and
to inhibit the development of homosexual love
triangles.[14] As with any "band-aid approach," however, the impact of the identification-isolation
method has been negligible. Even when the diagnostic tools used to identify and differentiate
between the institutional (situational) homosexual
and the aggressive practicing ("true") homosexual
have been fairly elaborate, their results have
fallen short of the expected goals. This is not
surprising, because this method does not attempt
to treat the environmental causes of institutional
homosexuality, and is not in line with the
seemingly valid premise that it is not the "true"
homosexual but the aggressive one who is really
the problem.

Another widely used approach, mentioned by
Richard Nice in "The Problems of Homosexuality in
Corrections," is

the use of group pressure and support and a
form of group therapy as an attempt to
modify homosexual ideation. Recent professional literature and a report by the American
Group Psychotherapy Association indicate that
37 per cent of homosexuals treated with the
minimum of twenty therapeutic sessions
"achieved an exclusive heterosexual adjustment, while 31 per cent were considered
improved and 31 per cent were considered
markedly improved."[15]

[14] Loren H. Roth, "Territoriality and homosexuality in a
male prison population," American Journal of Orthopsychi-
atry, 41 (3), 1971, pp. 510-513.

[15] Richard W. Nice, "The problems of homosexuality in
corrections," American Journal of Corrections, May-June,
1966, p. 32.

However, although group or individual psychotherapy can be quite an effective method of treatment for homosexuality in general, it usually
proves unsatisfactory in prison. Staffing shortages make intensive psychotherapeutic treatment
impractical in most cases. Moreover, like other
approaches, psychotherapy does not treat the
inmate's full environment and is not a preventive
measure.

Another approach to the problem of prison
homosexuality involves an organized effort to
redirect an inmate's sexual drives by providing
constructive activities in which he can become
involved. The advantage of offering activities
that reinforce male offenders' masculine strivings is pointed out by Buffum.

> The problem for the prison administrator
> . . . becomes considerably more complex than
> merely the suppression of sexual activity—
> it becomes a problem of providing those
> activities for which the homosexual contacts
> are serving as substitutes. The inmates are
> acting out their needs for self-expression,
> control over their own behavior, affection,
> and the stability of human relationships.
> The homosexual relationship provides one of
> the few powerful ways of expressing and
> gratifying these needs. Unless these needs
> are met in some other way, there is little
> opportunity for adequate control of homo-
> sexual activity in the prison environment.
>
> There are a variety of administrative
> policies and procedures which bear on the
> issue of inmate self-expression and self-
> determination. Good educational and
> vocational training programs and, in partic-
> ular, legitimate work opportunities will help
> to provide a focus for an identity or self-
> image which can be perceived as both power-
> ful and productive. Opportunities for
> inmates to participate within prison
> organizations, particularly in elected or

appointed positions, can also serve to
reinforce masculine strivings.[16]

Performing a homosexual act is often the offender's way of saying, "Sex is something I can still
control." By developing programs that allow the
inmate to exert initiative, keep active, and
demonstrate some control over his environment,
the psychologist might be taking one of the most
positive steps possible toward curbing prison
homosexuality.

Legal measures also may be used to deter homosexual behavior in general, and sexual attacks in
particular. As might be expected, though, this
approach is not used very often. Even in the case
of the extremely aggressive homosexual rapist,
where legal action is most desirable and effective, prosecution only results in a handful of
cases.

Probably the most controversial and publicized
solution to homosexuality problems in prison is
conjugal visits. Although this strategy of allowing wives more extensive visits with their
husbands has been widely debated in this country
for only a short time, it is not new and is used
considerably, especially outside the United States.

In India, Pakistan, Mexico's Penal Isle of
Marias, and the Philippines, some types of inmates
are permitted to invite their families to live on
the prison grounds with them. Hayner describes
the program in Mexico as follows:

The practice of conjugal visits in Mexican
prisons is a realistic method of meeting the
sex problem. Not only does it combat homosexuality; it often changes the entire
behavior of the convict. It should be remem-
bered that Mexico has a very strong family
tradition. Even more than in the United
States the family is regarded as a fundamental

[16] Buffum, op. cit., p. 29.

institution. Anything that tends to destroy the family meets with opposition; anything that strengthens it is supported. It is believed that the conjugal visit keeps couples together. When the manager of a Mexican hotel gave his assistant cook her free day on Thursday so that she could visit her husband in the local bastille that day, he was acting in harmony with Mexican mores.[17]

Conjugal visitation has also been in use for a long time in the United States, at least on an informal basis. At the Mississippi State Penitentiary, conjugal visits apparently have been an unofficial custom since the camp's origin in 1900.[18] However, there is still great opposition to this practice in this country. Some of the objections prison administrators express have been noted by Joseph Balogh. Some administrators, he found, are noncommittal, evasive, or defensive on the subject. Those who favor conjugal visits generally feel that the program "should be limited strictly to legally married male persons." The advantages of a conjugal visiting program are that it seems to help inmates preserve their family ties; it is more desirable than the sexual outlets available in prison; it gives inmates incentive; it reduces the number of escapes and escape attempts; and it improves prison morale. Those penal administrators who oppose conjugal visitations argue that it is too expensive; it encourages sexual immorality; its advocates are overly optimistic about its benefits; it creates an unfavorable public impression; it gives some prisoners preferential treatment that may have a negative effect; it magnifies custody and security

[17] Ruth S. Cavan and Eugene S. Zemans, "Marital relationship of prisoners in twenty-eight countries," Journal of Criminal Law, Criminology and Police Science, July-Aug., vol. 49, no. 2, 1958, p. 139.

[18] C. B. Hopper, "Conjugal visiting at the Mississippi state penitentiary," Federal Probation, vol. 28, 1964, pp. 40-41.

problems; and it can corrupt the prison staff.[19]
From Balogh's summary one can see that although
the concept of the conjugal visit offers promise,
administrators' objections to it indicate that,
like other solutions, it has some serious deficiencies.

A correctional worker interested in this area
adds the following criticism of conjugal visitations:

> Some people seem to believe that if a more
> intimate relationship was available it would
> greatly eliminate such things as homosexual-
> ity and tension within the institution. It
> has been our experience that when the man has
> good family relationships, a good stable home
> where both he and his wife are emotionally
> mature, there is no problem along these
> lines, even though this intimate relation-
> ship is not available. The true problem in
> regard to homosexuality and tension brought
> about by an unsatisfied sex drive, lies with
> the unstable immature individual who has
> been married numerous times and who
> possesses definite psychopathic personality
> traits. To offer a more intimate relation-
> ship to this type of individual would be
> ridiculous. We do not feel that a more
> intimate relationship between a man and his
> wife would eliminate many of our problems
> within our institution.[20]

One of the strongest and most sensible alternatives to the conjugal visiting approach is home
visits. Tom Clayton feels that in many ways it is

[19] Joseph K. Balogh, "Conjugal visitation in prisons: a
sociological perspective," Federal Probation, vol. 28,
1964, p. 58.

[20] Eugene S. Zemans and Ruth S. Cavan, "Marital relationships of prisoners," Journal of Criminal Law, Criminology and Police Science, May-June, vol. 49, no. 1, 1958,
p. 54.

more productive for a prisoner to visit his home
than try to recreate it behind bars.

> The one prison issue on which I found almost
> complete agreement on all sides was the ques-
> tion of allowing what staff referred to as
> 'conjugal visits' and prisoners as 'passion
> week-ends.' They were regarded as impracti-
> cal on moral, psychological and administra-
> tive grounds under existing prison conditions.
> The Advisory Council on the Penal System, who
> studied the regime for long-term prisoners in
> conditions of maximum security, said that
> 'very little is reliably established about
> sexuality in prison and the reactions of
> prisoners to sexual frustration.' It appeared
> to be in substantial agreement that 'conjugal
> visits' were impractical and to favour the
> granting of home leave visits to some prison-
> ers. 'One very relevant point is that home
> leave enables a man to resume contact not
> only with his wife but also with his chil-
> dren. If we are thinking of ways of keeping
> family relationships viable against release,
> the link between parent and child is as
> important as that between man and wife.
> Moreover, home leave can be granted to enable
> an unmarried prisoner to visit his parents or
> other relatives, and need not be confined to
> married men.'[21]

Conclusions

From the reports on prison sexuality discussed
thus far, two points seem evident: (1) no one
solution to the problem has proved totally effective, and (2) we still lack a concrete body of
knowledge in this area. To correct the latter
problem, studies on prison sexual careers should
be done to provide enough reliable information to
replace the current fragmentary assumptions about
homosexual activities in prison.

[21] Tom Clayton, Men in Prison, Hamish Hamilton, London,
1970, p. 188.

In response to the need for an immediate, effective way to deal with prison sexuality, pending the recommendations of future studies, Nice's suggestion "to combine several of the existing services now offered in a prison setting" appears to be a logical approach.[22] Yet, probably the most effective step we can take to handle prison sexuality is to continue encouraging humanization of oppressive prison settings by establishing constructive activities in which inmates can become involved.

A surprising number of inmates who have had homosexual contacts in prison resume a heterosexual existence when released into the free community. This movement away from homosexual behavior upon returning to the community seems to arise not only from the availability of members of the opposite sex, but also from an environment that allows former inmates freedom to influence their own destiny. If prisons continue to keep inmates in a dependent position, no other efforts—short of abolishing prisons entirely—will have any great impact on the frequency of prison homosexuality.

THE RELATIONSHIP BETWEEN TREATMENT AND CUSTODIAL STAFFS

The team concept for rehabilitating the offender is built on the assumption that custodial and treatment staffs work as a single, cooperating unit. Unfortunately, this is not always the case. In most penal settings, the custodial (uniformed, security) personnel and the treatment (civilian, rehabilitation) staffs are often at odds over correctional goals and the administrative procedures that should be used to deal with inmates' problems.

[22] Nice, op. cit., p. 32.

123

Unusual Problems

The Custodial Staff

Many custodial personnel are suspicious of the
civilians who come to visit or work in a prison.
As one senior correction officer (C.O.) stated,
"When a civilian would come into my institution,
I would always wonder what he wanted. I would
smile at him and be pleasant, but at the same time
I'd watch him closely to see what he was up to
because civilians usually mean nothing but
trouble."

The negative feelings of many C.O.'s toward
civilians result from bad experiences in which
civilians have taken inappropriate action during,
or following, a visit to a penal institution. In
some instances, a visiting civilian "expert" might
criticize the work or policy of the custodial
staff without taking into consideration the
limited resources at their disposal or the great
problems they face on the tiers. In the same
vein, a civilian worker might unknowingly violate
a good security principle and precipitate a situation that causes more work and trouble for the
C.O.

The C.O. may also hold general grudges against
civilians as a whole because of current trends in
corrections, which he feels undermine his authority. The movement to curtail the use of physical
force to control inmates is among the most noteworthy in this area. Many an officer can be
heard saying something like, "Ten years ago the
inmates weren't running this prison. In those
days you could smack them in the mouth if they
didn't listen."

Another problem which increases the dislike
the C.O. has for the treatment staff is based on
the educational differences between the two
staffs. The treatment personnel often lack
correctional experience, but usually have a
college education. With the officer, the situation is reversed. This gap should diminish as
the movement to encourage C.O.'s to continue with
college level courses becomes more widespread.

Adding to the division between treatment and custodial staffs is the difference in how they perceive their role. The C.O. usually sees himself more as a peace officer than as an agent of correctional rehabilitation. He shies away from associating with the ("do-gooder") mental health staff and associates himself instead with the police officer.

Several correction officers were asked if they perceived their role as expanding into a new form where they would work more actively with the rehabilitation personnel. The feelings they expressed indicated that they disliked the idea.

C.O. A.: "I don't want to be a psychiatric aide. I was hired to be a peace officer. The less I have to do with the mental health staff, the better I like it."

C.O. L.: "The psychological staff has its head in the clouds. They don't mix with the inmates on the tiers like I do, or they'd know you can't trust them."

C.O. R.: "I don't want to work with the mental health workers too closely. If we start that, soon we'll be taking orders from the doctors instead of one of our own people. Then before you know it, these shrinks will be replacing us. . . . I don't want any part of it."

The Treatment Staff

Many members of the rehabilitation staff (psychologists, medical doctors, mental health workers) have an equally negative view of the C.O. One of the reasons for this is the apparently arbitrary way that C.O.'s enforce institutional rules. While one C.O. may adhere strictly to the book, another may be quite permissive. A good example of this in most prisons is the regulation that each person must show his pass when he enters a facility. While one C.O. will not ask for it if he recognizes you, another might always demand to see it. Such variance in

the enforcement of the rules is often interpreted
by the treatment staff as harassment, causing
bitterness between the correctional officer and
the mental health worker.

Another element that separates the two groups
is the priority of correctional goals. The
uniformed force sees security as the top priority;
the treatment personnel consider the primary goal
to be rehabilitation.

Fanning this division is the antisocial manipulator. Such an inmate may go to a member of the
security force and try to gain favor with the
officer by saying something like, "The treatment
personnel are easy marks for the prisoners—
rehabilitation to us means just milking the
doctors for all the benefits we can get."

After doing this, the inmate might turn to a
member of the treatment staff and try to play on
his prejudice toward the custodial staff, saying,
"All the cops know is brutality." He might mention that the C.O. lacks a college education and
indicate that therefore the inmates naturally
respect the civilian more.

Correcting the Problem

To increase the overall effectiveness of the
correction team, the conflicts between the two
staffs must be reconciled. The three main steps
correctional personnel can take toward this goal
are improving relations between current staff
members, providing sensitivity training for new
employees in the area of staff relations, and
establishing new roles for the C.O. which would
involve treatment as well as custodial functions.

Group meetings for treatment and custodial
members together would be one way to start lessen-
ing the friction between these two groups. The
administration might also go over and clarify
institutional procedures, perhaps with the help
of both staffs. In too many facilities, the
security and treatment policies are passed on by

word of mouth. This is insufficient: They must be put in writing and given out to all personnel.

Orientation sessions for new custodial and civilian personnel should emphasize interdependency of the two staffs, as should the group meetings for staff already working in the prison. It is particularly important for the custodial personnel to see the rehabilitation staff as members of the team, instead of "outsiders," as they frequently do now. The C.O. should also realize that expanding his role by becoming involved with the treatment staff will contribute toward the professional status of his position. At a time when correction officers are concerned about being replaced by a "fleet of mental health personnel," this point should be encouraging.

Whatever steps are taken, the important point is that the directors of both institutional staffs must realize that some action is necessary to close the gap between the two groups. Treatment must be made the job of both custodial and rehabilitation staffs, and this can be done without unnecessary violations of sound security principles.

The dual problem of confining and rehabilitating the offender is a frustrating enough job. Destructive staff rivalry only drains an institution's resources. Innovative therapy and increased funds can have little impact until the effort wasted in staff power plays is diverted back to the real goals of the institution. It is therefore evident that improving working relationships between the custodial and treatment staffs should be one of the top priorities in the correctional facility.

Unusual Problems

CORE REFERENCES

Sex Offenders

Gebhard, Paul, Gagnon, John, Pomeroy, Wardell, and Christenson, Cornelia. Sex Offenders. New York: Harper & Row, 1965.
The results of a study, based on personal interviews with more than 1,500 convicted sex offenders, to determine whether—and how—persons who have been imprisoned for various sex offenses differ from other inmates, and how they differ from one another.

Prison Sexuality

Buffum, Peter C. Homosexuality in Prisons. Washington, D.C.: U.S. Dept. of Justice, 1972.
An excellent discussion of the problem of homosexuality in penal institutions.

CHAPTER 8

Programs for
the Offender

When an offender is sent to prison, it is with at
least the implicit assumption that he will be
participating in some type of rehabilitative program while in confinement. Though many of the
programs now in existence have met with only
limited success, some of the more innovative ones
do offer promise. These approaches can be grouped
and typed as being either recreational, vocational,
or educational.

RECREATION IN CORRECTIONAL INSTITUTIONS

Appropriate health care for the offender means
more than just tending to his illnesses or
injuries. Psychological and medical authorities
now recognize that recreation, thought by many to
be an unimportant sideline to the other "more
meaningful" programs, is crucial to rehabilitation. Good recreation programs can prevent the
boring, depressing, and frustrating institutional
environment from taking its toll on the offender's
mental health. A good athletic program, for
example, can provide an incentive for good conduct, be a positive outlet for physical energy,
and generally improve both mental health and
interpersonal relations.

Programs for the Offender

The value of structured recreation as a treatment tool in corrections was demonstrated at the
Robert F. Kennedy Youth Center, where the treatment staff used operant shaping techniques in
conjunction with basketball games. Games were
scheduled between mature youths and antisocial
delinquents. When the delinquents behaved acceptably during the game, the staff rewarded them with
approval and permission to play in subsequent
games. The first game was marked by verbal abuse,
temper tantrums, and physical assaults. By the
final game, however, the delinquents were controlling their behavior.[1]

Recreation can also make diagnosis easier.
During free time activities, the psychologist is
able to observe an aspect of inmate behavior that
is not visible at other times. And if inmates are
involved in the actual planning of their recreational program, as in Maine State Prison, this
affords a further opportunity for the psychologist to evaluate the offenders' levels and styles
of interpersonal relations.[2]

Recreation activities can ease re-entry into
the community as well. The Camp Flambeau Project
gave juvenile offenders an opportunity to participate in local softball leagues. This chance to
interact with the peers they would come into
contact with upon release helped the youths to
adjust to society.[3]

[1]Gilbert L. Ingram and John A Minor, "Shaping the
recreational behavior of psychopathic delinquents," Journal
of Correctional Education, 22 (3), 1970, pp. 24-26.

[2]Maine State Prison, Synopsis of Current Programs,
1970.

[3]Wisconsin Corrections Division, Camp Flambeau Project,
Madison, 1971.

Approaches other than athletics have also been applied by correction workers. At the Bryn-y-Don School in England, drama was used as a creative evening activity to help the boys to become more observant of themselves and of those around them.[4] Writing is also achieving limited results; it seems to give inmates an opportunity to express their creative abilities. At the State Prison of South Michigan, more than 200 inmates have sent out manuscripts for consideration by non-institutional periodicals.[5] And in California, Project Unity arranges for rock and folk performers to give concerts in prisons.

Dance is another recreational activity that has been tried in the penal setting. In an attempt to test the hypothesis that dance experiences can produce desirable changes in the behavior of female prisoners, 36 inmates at the Goree Unit of the Texas Department of Correction were selected to participate in an experimental dance class. Twenty-four of the original 36 inmates remained in the class at the end of the experimental period. During the course of the program, the inmates taking part visited the prison hospital less frequently than usual. They reported fewer feelings of depression, less tension from constant supervision, and less resentment of authority. In addition, the inmates showed improved sleeping habits and fewer spells of uncontrollable laughing and crying.[6]

[4]Gerry Attrill, "Drama as an evening activity," Community Schools Gazette, 64 (9), 1970, pp. 509-512.

[5]Ernest C. Brooks, "Something new in prison responsibility," American Journal of Correction, 27 (1), 1965, pp. 14-16.

[6]Mary Ella Montague, "The effects of dance experiences upon observable behaviors of women prisoners," submitted in partial fulfillment of the requirements for the degree of Doctor of Education in the School of Education of New York University, 1961.

Recreational activities help many offenders by training them to use their leisure time constructively upon release. The individual involved in crime, especially the drug addict, often has not learned, or has forgotten, how to spend his waking, non-working hours in a socially acceptable manner. Boredom easily can lead to a decision to perform a criminal act. Therefore, the inmate who has become interested in a constructive leisure time activity can avoid destructive idleness while incarcerated, and will be prepared for release into a community where the free time allotted to the average worker is on the increase.

VOCATIONAL TRAINING FOR OFFENDERS

Vocational training is one of the most traditionally acceptable methods of correcting offenders. It is a long-standing belief that a man with a trade can get a decent job, and a person with a good job does not need to steal. Recent studies, however, have cast some doubt on the validity of this assumption. A study at the California Institute for Women indicated that vocational training did not affect the frequency of inmates' violations.[7] Another report by the Washington State Division of Program Evaluation and Statistics found no significant difference in the recidivism rate between inmates who completed vocational training and those who did not.[8]

Since the criteria used in these studies— recidivism and parole outcome—are related to goals that training alone cannot hope to achieve,

[7]William R. Conte, "Correctional education—a many-faceted thing," Journal of Correctional Education, vol. 19, no. 4, 1967, pp. 10-11.

[8]Carol Spencer and John E. Berecochea, "Vocational training at the California Institute for Women: an evaluation," Research Report No. 41, Research Division, California Department of Corrections, 1971, pp. 29-33.

the conclusion that vocational training is not
having much impact may be misleading. Vocational
programs are only part of the overall rehabilitative effort and cannot be saddled with the full
responsibility for an offender's failure or
success after release. At the very least, though,
these reports point out a need to examine the
whole vocational training process to see if this
"sacred cow" in corrections is functioning as
effectively as some believe it is.

Institutional Work

Prison work has a twofold purpose: rehabilitating the offender by giving him an opportunity
to learn a trade, and producing goods and
services needed by the prison or community at a
saving to the taxpayers. In the past, unfortunately, producing goods economically and performing routine prison functions at a low cost have
become more important to many prison officials
than providing worthwhile work experience for the
incarcerated offender. Inmates are often
recruited to perform menial institutional functions with little vocational value, under the
guise of special on-the-job training.

In response to this situation, some administrators have tried to involve inmates less in
institutional needs, and gear their training more
toward gaining knowledge and skills that will be
useful to them. In addition, steps have been
taken to improve the process of selecting inmates
for training, increase offenders' motivation to
work, develop programmed instruction packages,
and break down community barriers against employing offenders.

Inmate Selection

One of the deficiencies in prisoner training
has been the process of selecting inmates for the
program. Instead of choosing an inmate for vocational training on the basis of his ability to
benefit from it, seniority, docility and expenda-
bility from prison work gangs have often been the

sole criteria. Such a policy could cause even the most advanced rehabilitation program to fail.

Motivation To Work

An offender's attitude and motivation are other main determinants of a program's success rate. An inmate who does not appreciate the value of the skills offered to help him become a self-supporting, independent human being will rarely put them to work in the community. Ideally, the inmate should accept responsibility for his own rehabilitation and recognize the need for change if his treatment is to be successful. If he does not have such a constructive attitude, and it cannot be instilled in him, all vocational efforts will fall short of their goals.

A study by the Michigan Corrections Department reported that no single policy change or program renovation improved inmates' use of the training programs available in prison once they were released. The researchers felt that it was not the training programs themselves that needed to be improved, but the prisoners' attitudes toward their working situation.[9] Unfortunately, as Dickover, Maynard, and Painter point out, most of the inmates in job training programs come from disadvantaged cultures that often discourage a job-oriented motivation. If this problem is not considered, vocational training will have little benefit for most of the population for whom it is intended.[10]

Programmed Instruction

In some cases, offenders lack the motivation to learn vocational skills because of learning

[9]Michigan Corrections Department, "The use of correctional trade training," 1969.

[10]Robert M. Dickover, Verner E. Maynard, and James A. Painter, "Motivational problems in vocational education," A Study of Vocational Training in the California Corrections Department, 1971.

difficulties. One of the ways correctional educators are dealing with this is by using programmed instructional techniques. Programmed material allows the student to proceed at his own pace, and rewards each small gain as he advances.

This technique was tested in an experiment at the Draper Correctional Center. The self-instruction school included a curriculum of 350 courses; there were 85 students, a cadre of academically advanced inmates, and four college students who helped the supervisor. McKee and Seay report that this experiment and others like it have succeeded in raising the students' scores on achievement tests, and that the offenders taking part were enthusiastic about the approach. [11]

Part of the problem with teaching inmates, like any other students, has been the difficulty of finding a program that is neither too demanding nor too simple for them. If the initial work is too hard, they will become discouraged and lose interest; if the tasks are made less complex, they may degenerate into "work-play" that hardly benefits the inmate at all. As a result, programmed instruction, which adapts to all levels and thus can reach even the intellectually disadvantaged, offers correctional educators cause for guarded optimism.

[11] John M. McKee and Donna M. Seay, "The Draper Experiment: a dramatic use of programmed instruction in a prison for youthful offenders," paper presented at the Conference on Programmed Learning and Electronic Media in Educational and Training Systems of the Detroit Society for Programmed Instruction, January 28, 1965. Also, Draper Correctional Center, "Experiences of the Draper E & D Project for the OMAT Program-Operation Retrieval: Youth," Elmore, Alabama.

Programs for the Offender

Non-institutional Barriers to Offender Employment

Even if a facility provides programmed instruction or other high quality prevocational training, and has a realistic overall vocational program, non-institutional barriers can still frustrate its efforts to place offenders in jobs. One of the worst of these problems is the lack of qualified staff to find jobs for parolees. Another difficulty is the gap between institutional and post-release training programs—many confinees need further structured training after they have been released into the community. Other serious blocks to inmate employment include union regulations, the stigma of a prison record, laws and regulations that limit the occupations in which ex-offenders may be licensed, and the low wages offered most former inmates.

To overcome such barriers to inmate employment, many recommendations—including a sweeping one that would phase out correctional industries and replace them with private industry[12]—have been made and are being considered. Although many efforts to make vocational training realistic have met with only marginal success thus far, at least the problems in this area are being faced. The maxim that "vocational training in any form benefits the inmate" is no longer accepted in corrections. Reaching this point has taken a long time. Now that vocational programs are open to critical examination, progress should be swifter in the future than it has been in the past.

CORRECTIONAL EDUCATION

Correctional education has progressed rapidly in the past five decades. In 1931, a survey of

[12] California State Assembly, "Report on the economic status and rehabilitation value of California correctional industries," 1969.

the nation's prisons done by Austin MacCormick indicated that none of them had a well-rounded and adequate educational system.[13] Now a number of institutional programs are refined and extensive enough to invalidate this 50-year-old report. The current status of prison education is still bleak enough, though, to prompt Chief Justice Warren Burger to say, "Today the programs of (correctional) education range from nonexistent to inadequate, with all too few exceptions."[14]

Short-Term Confinement Facilities

The shortage of educational programs is probably most evident in the jail or short-term confinement facility. The 1970 National Jail Census of the Law Enforcement Assistance Administration noted that 90 percent of the jails in the U.S. had no educational programs at all.[15]

Local departments of correction can change, and should, so that inmates awaiting trial can work toward constructive goals. Even institutions where confinees remain for an average of less than a month can provide some form of educational program. The City-County Workhouse in St. Paul, Minnesota, for example, offers inmates both an approved high school equivalency test and

[13] Austin H. MacCormick, The Education of Adult Prisoners, a Survey and a Program, The National Society of Penal Information, New York, 1931.

[14] We Hold These Truths, National Conference on Corrections, Williamsburg, Virginia, December 5-8, 1971. Remarks of U.S. Chief Justice Warren E. Burger, pp. 5-12.

[15] "Local adult correctional institutions and jails," from the report of the President's Commission on Law Enforcement and Administration of Justice, Washington, D.C., U.S. Government Printing Office, 1967, pp. 162-169.

intensive training to prepare for the test.[16]
Another of the few jails in the nation that have
set up educational programs is the District of
Columbia jail. Between 1968 and 1971, nearly 300
inmates were given literacy training or remedial
education, worked for a high school equivalency
certificate, or took college-level correspondence
courses.[17]

Lack of Resources

Two of the most significant problems with
correctional education today are lack of staff and
inadequate library facilities. John Glenn, study-
ing the educational programs at Arizona State,
concluded that even if an appreciable number of
inmates could be persuaded to participate in a
program, present staffing could not meet their
educational needs.[18] In response to this shortage,
some systems have turned to the better qualified
inmates for teachers. Naturally, some correctional administrators have reservations about such
a procedure.

> We feel that an inmate teacher cannot possibly
> supply the motivation, set the kind of
> example, or provide the sort of image which
> is necessary if education is to be meaning-
> ful.[19]

[16] Lucille E. Blank, "Education in a short-term institution," American Journal of Correction, 28 (6), 1966,
pp. 21-23.

[17] District of Columbia, Corrections Department, The
Educational Program of the D.C. Jail: Analysis and
Recommendations, by Ann Jacobs, Stuart Adams, and Bernard
Schultz, 1971.

[18] John Glenn, Correctional Programs in Education, for
the Arizona Department of Corrections, 1969, p. 54.

[19] Steven P. Schwartz, Daniel A. Sisneros, and William D.
Smith, with the resident students of the Penitentiary
Community College of Santa Fe, with the aid and direction

Administrators' concern about using inmates to train other inmates seems reasonable, for even trained and certified correctional educators need abilities beyond those of the community classroom instructor to be effective in the correctional setting. Therefore, the instructor should be familiar not only with his primary subject area, but also with the special topics of crime and delinquency. Further, he must be flexible enough to meet his students' needs despite the fact that they might vary greatly. Other pressures the teacher has to deal with include the lack of motivation among many offenders because of past experiences of failure, the antisocial tendencies of some prisoners, and the lack of warmth and personal concern in the institutional setting.

The correctional psychologist often relies on the teacher to assist in rehabilitating inmates. Therefore, the teacher is expected to be able to accept and respect delinquents and help provide an environment in which they will not feel a need to battle, but will be able to relate to, identify with, and learn from their teachers and peers. Realistically, however, most teachers in prisons in the United States do not have these traits, and many of them also lack the motivation to function as effective members of the treatment team. Usually, prisons are the "catch-all" for the inexperienced, underqualified, or unrealistically motivated teacher. This is not always the case, but it seems to hold true for a majority of our prisons.

Another grossly inadequate area in prison education is the limited library facilities usually available to inmates. An institutional library can provide general, technical, and occupational information. It may help the offender

of Joseph F. Sneed, From Prison to Classroom II: a report to the five sponsoring agencies of a paraprofessional teacher training program at the Penitentiary of New Mexico, Part 1, p. 1, 1972.

to develop reading as a leisure time activity, aid him in releasing tension, and prepare him for post-release life. Ideally, a good library program can motivate the illiterate inmate to become literate, and it can supplement the institution's overall educational program. But like staff shortages, limited library facilities can also prevent an otherwise effective educational program from achieving its potential.

PROGRESS IN CORRECTIONAL EDUCATION

In addition to the shortage of capable prison educators and adequate library facilities, many prisons have too few instructional materials to meet the inmate population's varied needs. This lack forces all students, no matter what their level of intelligence and achievement, to proceed at the same pace. The answer to this problem, as in the area of vocational training, may be the use of programmed instruction. This technique can compensate for many of the deficiencies in prison academic programs by providing material that is geared to meet different needs.

Programmed instruction seems particularly useful with inmates whose English is awkward or inadequate, since it minimizes the need for competence in spoken English for the beginning student. Furthermore, by allowing the student to proceed at his own pace and rewarding him with positive feedback when he answers questions correctly, programmed instruction encourages students to expect success rather than failure, and offers them immediate satisfaction with their progress. Also, fewer teachers are needed with programmed materials than with other kinds of instruction. Further, this method avoids creating a destructive level of competition, since it is based on a self-study, self-testing philosophy.

Institutional Support

Another essential ingredient for the success of a correctional education program is a positive attitude on the part of administration. One study attributed most of the difficulties in fitting the Upward Bound program into the Oregon Prison System to a lack of communication between prison and Upward Bound personnel and administration.[20] With the proper support, however, correctional education seems to have a good chance of achieving several goals: It can improve the offender's self-image and his attitude toward others, increase his level of achievement, overcome his negative view of education, and teach him enough competence in language and basic academic skills to help him find a productive place in society.[21]

HIGHER EDUCATION IN CORRECTIONAL INSTITUTIONS

As in the case of secondary-level education in corrections, the status of higher education at present is unimpressive. Though the current trend to create college-level education programs in correctional institutions is broad, it is still fairly superficial.[22]

[20] Oregon State Board of Control, Corrections Division, An Evaluation of the Upward Bound Oregon Prison Project, 1968.

[21] California Youth Authority, Compensatory Education in the California Youth Authority, 1969-1970, Sacramento, 1970. Also, John F. Hughes, Title I ESEA in Institutions for Neglected and Delinquent Children, U.S. Department of Health, Education, and Welfare, Washington, D.C., 1967. Also, Daniel Glaser, "The effectiveness of correctional education," American Journal of Correction, 28 (2), 1966, pp. 4-9.

[22] Albert R. Roberts, "Current trends in college-level instruction for inmates of correctional institutions," Journal of Correctional Education, 21 (4), 1969, pp. 34-37.

Programs for the Offender

College-level courses have been offered to inmates since as early as 1932. College correspondence courses have been available since at least 1934.[23] However, what seems to be the first full college program in a prison has only been in operation since 1952, when the Illinois State Penitentiary at Menard established it in conjunction with Southern Illinois University. The program at Menard developed to the point that in 1962 college-credit courses were offered to almost 30 inmates, who were excused from prison work to pursue an academic load equal to that of full-time students in the community.[24]

Current Status

C. A. Laird found in a 1970 survey that correctional facilities in 35 states were offering college-level programs. Four forms of instruction were used in these settings: live instruction, correspondence courses, television hook-ups, and releasing inmates to outside educational facilities.[25]

Laird found that live instruction seems to be on the rise. "Twenty-six state institutions and 10 federal units reported enrollment in live instruction. Total enrollment in live instruction by 1970 equalled 2,878 students in state programs and 683 in federal prisons."[26] In

[23] C. A. Laird, "A study of the college level education program of the Texas Department of Corrections," Ph.D. thesis, University of Houston, 1971. Also, Delyte Morris, "The university's role in prison education," Nebraska Law Review, 45 (3), 1966, pp. 542-571.

[24] Craig Calvin, "The role of higher education in the rehabilitation of the public offender," paper presented to the Canadian Congress of Criminology and Corrections in Ottawa, Canada, June 13-18, 1971, p. 6. Also, Eugene Doleschal, "Higher education in U.S. prisons," Information Review on Crime and Delinquency, vol. 1, no. 1, 1968, p. 2.

[25] C. A. Laird, op. cit.   [26] Ibid., p. 4.

addition, study-release and school furlough programs seem to be expanding, which is not surprising in view of the trend toward community-based
corrections. Another advantage to inmate educational programs outside the institution, as Kerle
notes, is that "education in an institutional
setting like a prison is continually hampered by
a number of problems, most of them human. Too
much goes on in the way of the educating
process."[27]

Sample Modern Programs

One unique college-level program was initiated
at the State Prison in Trenton, New Jersey, with
the assistance of Mercer County Community College.
It started in 1968 as a part-time college program,
and since then it has grown to over five times its
original size in curriculum and enrollment.
Courses in the full-time program include ethics,
Afro-American history, history of western civili-
zation, biology, and psychology. In 1971 the
program added a special prison education communication network that was designed by New Jersey
Bell to the specifications of instructors at
Mercer. The set-up enables professors to teach
the students at the prison and those on campus the
same course at the same time. As the prisoner
hears the professor's voice, an electrowriter (a
two-way communication hookup) projects the professor's writing onto a screen at the prison. Two-
way microphones allow the students at the prison
to question both the students and the professor
on campus.[28]

[27] Kenneth E. Kerle, "Inmate education: U.S. and
Europe," address given at the American Association for the
Advancement of Science, 139th meeting, Dec. 30, 1972,
p. 20.

[28] David A. Willetts, "The college behind bars," Welfare
Reporter, 22 (3), 1971, pp. 19-21. Also, "College behind
bars," Communications for Business, Winter 1972, pp. 2-7.

Programs for the Offender

    The San Quentin Prison College Project was
inaugurated in 1966 with funding from a Ford
Foundation grant. This project was set up by the
University of California at Berkeley and the
California Department of Correction with the goal
of establishing an accredited four-year college
program within the correctional system.

    As the first step in the project, a question-
naire was distributed within San Quentin. 1,093
inmates returned it; 629 inmates, or about one-
sixth of the prison population, expressed interest
in the project. Inmates were admitted to the
program if they had a high school diploma and if
they made an acceptable impression in a pre-
enrollment interview. They could register in
eight courses or programs, including criminology;
114 students enrolled, and four classes were
formed. After the program proceeded successfully
through five terms, its directors developed plans
for an Associate of Arts degree program at San
Quentin, where inmates could earn a degree in five
semesters.

    As a result of this project's progress, its
proponents claim they have demonstrated several
important points:

    1. A meaningful program in higher education
can be carried on in a major prison.

    2. Inmates without prior college instruction
perform as well as or better than outside students
who enroll in the same courses as part of a full
college program.

    3. Participation in the program can lead to
conspicuous changes in the attitudes, behavior,
and career plans of some participants, a higher
interest in improving the quality of prison life,
and a weakened identification with deviant
behavior.

    On the basis of their experience with this
project, the psychologists and educators involved
also made several recommendations regarding

post-secondary education in the correctional
setting. They felt that (1) college programs in
prisons should be organized primarily around the
two-year degree, but should provide ample opportunity for studies at higher levels; (2) college
programs should be regarded as instruments for
effecting change not only in participants but in
other inmates and staff as well; (3) the college
career of the inmate should be flexible and
should include both a segment of education in
prison and another in the outside academic community; (4) correctional workers should experiment
with the "sentence to college" concept, by which
selected offenders would be placed in "halfway-in"
centers after being screened shortly after
incarceration. These offenders would remain under
supervision, with attendance in classes being a
primary obligation.[29]

Project NewGate, started in 1967 as a modification of the Upward Bound Oregon Prison Project,
was developed by Gaddis, author of Birdman of
Alcatraz, at the Oregon State Penitentiary. He
designed it to develop and demonstrate new
methods of integrating the offender into society,
with emphasis on higher education and counseling.[30]

By 1971, six NewGates had been established in
Oregon, Colorado, Kentucky, Minnesota, New Mexico,
and Pennsylvania. NewGate is considered unique
by its users because it links three therapeutic
components into a single extensive program:
guidance and counseling within the institution,
post-secondary education within the institution,
and continuation of both the counseling and education programs outside the institution. In essence,
NewGate's operating principle is to bring community facilities and people into the correctional

[29] Stuart Adams, "The San Quentin Prison College Project:
final report, phase 1," University of California at
Berkeley, 1968.

[30] John J. Marsh, "The educator's mission impossible,"
Educational Media, 3 (6), 1971, pp. 6, 17.

program, and to extend the prison's educational
and counseling resources to community-based
systems into which student-inmates can move upon
release. [31]

Although such projects as NewGate and the ones
at San Quentin and Trenton State point to an
expanding acceptance of college-level programs in
corrections, there are still some community prejudices against the inmate or ex-offender as a
student. A study done recently by McCabe and
Driscoll to check college admission practices in
regard to ex-offenders uncovered a bias against
enrolling former inmates. While a majority of
the 705 schools that responded (response rate to
the questionnaire was only 32%) were willing to
accept certain types of offenders, a good number
noted that they considered an applicant's prior
criminal record in making their admissions decisions. [32]

A more serious problem than admission bias is
the failure of many post-secondary programs to
link up the educational part of the overall
rehabilitation process with institutional counseling, job placement, and post-release guidance and
therapy. Though some programs, such as NewGate,
do provide multidisciplinary treatment, they still
are in the minority.

Higher education, like such other types of
programs as vocational and recreational ones,
have long been unfairly criticized for their
failure to reduce recidivism. Critics often fail
to consider that a reeducation program is only

[31] National Council on Crime and Delinquency, "NewGate:
new hope through education," NCCD, Paramus, New Jersey.

[32] Patrick M. McCabe and Brian Driscoll, "College
admission opportunities and the public offender," paper
presented to the American Association of College Admission
Counselors, Sept. 30, 1971, San Francisco, California,
p. 19.

part of a total treatment plan. No vocational, recreational, or educational program in itself will stop recidivism. If such a program is not conceived and applied as one section of a broad socio-psycho-medical approach, it will probably have little long-range impact and ultimately will be condemned for its "failure" as a correctional method. Yet, as more and more comprehensive and multidisciplinary treatment programs emerge, their coordinators and evaluators finally may see the positive results they desire.

CORE REFERENCES

Kerle, Kenneth E. "Inmate education: U.S. and Europe." Paper presented at the American Association for the Advancement of Science, 139th meeting, Dec. 30, 1972.
A comprehensive discussion of trends in inmate education.

Marsh, John J. "Higher education in American prisons," Crime and Delinquency Literature, March, 1973, vol. 5, no. 1, pp. 139-155.
An article dealing with post-secondary education for criminal offenders.

Roberts, Albert R. "Recreation in correctional institutions," in Sourcebook on Prison Education: Past, Present, and Future. Charles C. Thomas, Springfield, 1971, pp. 150-161.
A brief treatment of correctional recreational programs.

For additional references, the Journal of Correctional Education should prove quite helpful.

CHAPTER 9

Community-Based
Corrections

Until fairly recently, most people felt that a secure institution was the proper environment in which to attempt to correct offenders. Even those humanitarians concerned with "cruel and unusual" prison conditions seldom favored community alternatives to imprisonment. Instead, they crusaded for more sensible and humane correctional facilities.

This philosophy is not generally held today, however. As Nora Klapmuts of the National Council on Crime and Delinquency points out,

> The distinctive characteristic of the current reform effort is its emphasis on abolishing rather than improving the prison. . . . In the light of criminological theory of the past decade, which views crime and delinquency as symptoms of disorganization of the community as much as of individual personalities—or even as a product of an inadequate mesh between the two—imprisonment is coming to be viewed as hopelessly anachronistic. It is now widely believed that reintegration of the offender with the law-abiding community—the primary goal of the "new" correction—cannot be accomplished

by isolating the offender in an artificial, custodial setting.[1]

COMMUNITY VERSUS INSTITUTIONAL TREATMENT

This movement to treat the offender in the community received great impetus in 1967, when the President's Commission on Law Enforcement and Administration of Justice took the position that "the goal of reintegration is likely to be furthered much more readily by working with offenders in the community than by incarceration."[2] The Commission took this stand partly because the cost of institutional treatment was rapidly increasing, while its benefits were still questionable. Their research indicated that community programs are not only much less costly on the whole than imprisonment, they also seem to be at least as effective in reducing recidivism.

Besides being expensive and uneven in its effectiveness, institutionalization also may have a destructive impact on the inmate. Even when the correctional facility's physical plant is set up to provide as therapeutic an environment as possible, the interruption of an offender's occupational and social life may destroy his chances of readjusting properly to society. As the President's Crime Commission stated, "Institutions tend to isolate offenders from society, both physically and psychologically, cutting them off from schools, jobs, families, and other supportive influences and increasing the probability that the label of criminal will be indelibly impressed upon them."[3]

[1]Nora Klapmuts, "Community alternatives to prison," Crime and Delinquency Literature, June, 1973, p. 305.

[2]President's Commission on Law Enforcement and Administration of Justice, The Challenge of Crime in a Free Society, U.S. Government Printing Office, 1967, p. 165.

[3]Ibid., p. 160.

With the disadvantages of institutionalization in mind, the Commission noted several types
of community programs that seemed likely to offer
practical and effective alternatives to incarceration. These were guided group interaction programs, foster homes and group homes, halfway
houses, intensive treatment programs, and reception center parole. All these approaches seem to
be worth using and testing to see if they can
serve as effective segments of the overall community offender treatment plan.

GUIDED GROUP INTERACTION (GGI)

Of the nonresidential programs they have been
examining, correctional psychologists and penologists have shown particular interest in the ones
involving GGI. As we discussed in Chapter 3,
proponents of GGI believe in involving the offender
in frequent, prolonged, intensive group discussions
of his behavior and that of his peers. This concept was first put into practice as early as 1950,
with the initiation of the Highfields project in
New Jersey. At Highfields, the group leader
encourages the youths to examine their immediate
experiences and problems, assume responsibility
for their own and other group members' actions,
and ultimately reach a point where they can share
decision-making powers with the staff.

Highfields treats up to 20 boys aged 16 and
17, with no record of former commitments to
correctional schools and no evidence of mental
retardation or severe physical disease. These
youths are assigned directly from the juvenile
court, with the expectation that they can be substantially rehabilitated within three to four
months (approximately half the average period of
incarceration in the State of New Jersey training
schools).

Highfields' house rules are not rigid, but
the youths do follow a basic schedule. During the
day they work at a mental institution next door to

151

the residence; at night they participate in group counseling sessions. They clean house on Saturday morning and have Saturday afternoon free, with Sunday left open to allow for visitors and religious observations. With this schedule as a framework and GGI as its primary therapeutic approach, Highfields "was at least as effective as the reformatory, perhaps more effective, and . . . accomplished its results in a much shorter period of time at greatly reduced costs," according to the Commission.[4] The project's long-range impact on recidivism is still uncertain, but at least to a limited extent, Highfields can be viewed as a successful community approach.

Other GGI Programs

With the innovative techniques employed at Highfields as a guide, variations of the GGI-based approach were initiated at Essexfields in New Jersey, and Pinehills in Provo, Utah. These projects were similar to Highfields in that their programs incorporated responsible employment in the community, school, and daily group meetings. However, in these two community experiments the offenders continued to live at home.

> The regimen at both Essexfields and Pinehills was rigorous. At Pinehills, for example, all boys were employed by the city. They put in a full day's work on the city streets, on the golf course, in the cemetery, wherever they were needed. They were paid 50 cents an hour. During the late afternoon, after the day's work was finished, all boys returned to the program headquarters where they met in daily group sessions. About 7 p.m. they were free to return home. They were also free on Sundays.

[4] President's Commission on Law Enforcement and Administration of Justice, Task Force Report: Corrections, U.S. Government Printing Office, 1967, p. 39.

In the daily group session all group
members, not just adult staff, were
responsible for defining problems and
finding solutions to them. By making
the program operations to some extent
the work of all involved, both offenders
and staff, it was possible to make a
better estimate of just how much responsibility for his own life a given offender
could take.

The fact that these guided group interaction programs are located in the community means that the problems with which
the group struggles are those that confront them daily in contact with their
families, friends, teachers, and employers.
This is one strength of a community program over an institutional one. The
artificiality of institutional life is
avoided, and concentration can be placed
upon the issues with which every offender
eventually has to deal.[5]

Pinehills' report of progress was particularly
closely examined since they were one of the first
community experiments to employ a research design
to assess program effectiveness statistically.
The results on one of the criteria used (recidivism) are contained in Table 1.

[5]Ibid., p. 39.

Community-Based Corrections

TABLE 1. Effectiveness of three programs for
juvenile delinquents, Utah, 1964, as measured
by percentages of releases not arrested within
6 months of release.

Program	Percentage of releasees not arrested within 6 months	
	All boys assigned to program	All boys completing program
Pinehills (experimental)	73	84
Probation (control)	73	77
State school (control)	42	42

Source: President's Commission, Task Force Report:
Corrections, 1967.

    While Table 1 indicates that the special
impact of GGI programs on recidivism is uncertain,
since there are no noteworthy differences between
the probation and Pinehills programs, the findings
do indicate that a community approach can be more
effective than costly incarceration in a state
school. And although other studies have not found
guided group interaction more effective than
incarceration[6] (possibly reflecting a selection
bias in the Pinehills program), most results did
demonstrate that this type of intervention in the
community is at least as effective as incarceration. Considering the high cost and usually
abnormal conditions involved in imprisonment,
this is certainly a positive finding.

    [6]Saul Pilnick et al., Collegefields: From Delin-
quency to Freedom, Newark State College, Newark, New
Jersey, 1967.

FOSTER HOMES AND GROUP HOMES

Probably the most traditional and widely accepted alternative to institutionalization for juvenile offenders has been foster home placement. According to the National Survey of Corrections, 42 percent of the 233 probation departments surveyed use foster homes, as do many juvenile aftercare programs.[7] Foster homes offer several theoretical advantages: they keep offenders in their own communities, and carry less stigma and cost less than imprisonment. Nevertheless, J. Robert Weber reported, "Discussions with State administrators would seem to indicate that foster care is in an eclipse. Reception center staffs report disillusionment with foster care for delinquents."[8] There appear to be two main problems: On the one hand, severing the family ties of those delinquents safe enough to remain in the community by sending them to a foster home is a poor choice if the alternative of probation at home is open. On the other, youths who are too unmanageable to remain at home are likely to be too disruptive for foster homes to deal with as well.

It is not surprising, then, that the group home concept is being considered by many correctional systems for youths who need a semi-institutional regimen and have a poor family-neighborhood environment. Two states moving in this direction are Minnesota and Wisconsin. Delinquents can be assigned the group home programs in Wisconsin either from the courts or from institutions; in Minnesota, placement is made only by court commitment.

[7]President's Commission, Task Force Report: Corrections, p. 40.

[8]J. Robert Weber, "A Report of the juvenile institutions project," unpublished report to the Osborne Association at the NCCD, September, 1966, p. 173.

Community-Based Corrections

The Youth Commission of Minnesota reported using seven group homes under arrangements with individual home operators or an intermediary agency. The payment plan was as follows: A nominal retaining fee was paid for each bed licensed, and when a youth actually took residence, the rate of pay was increased. Under a similar plan, the Wisconsin Department of Corrections operated 33 homes, with four to eight adolescents in each home.[9]

In addition to these programs, one of the most ambitious group programs to date is the Silverlake Experiment in Los Angeles. In this project, a large family home in a middle-class neighborhood was used as the treatment center and residence for up to 20 delinquent boys, ages 16 to 18. The youths lived at the house during the week, attended school daily, and lived at home on the weekends. A group meeting was held every day to provide a forum in which staff and residents could share information about problem behavior. These daily sessions also helped group members to develop responsibility and learn to exert proper social control of themselves and their peers within the program culture.[10]

Probationed Offenders Rehabilitation Training (PORT)

PORT was established in 1969 to serve three counties in southern Minnesota, as a live-in, community-based, community-supported treatment program for both adult offenders and juvenile delinquents. According to PORT's former director,

[9]Communication from Keith Griffiths, Chief, Division of Research, California Youth Authority, December, 1966, to President's Commission on Law Enforcement and the Administration of Justice.

[10]LaMar T. Empey and George E. Newland, "Staff-inmate collaboration: a study of critical incidents and consequences in the Silverlake experiment," Journal of Research in Crime and Delinquency, 5 (1), pp. 1-17, 1968.

it was designed as "an alternative for those offenders—currently only male—who require a greater change in their lifestyle than probation can accomplish and who, except for PORT, would end up in a prison or training school."[11]

The PORT facility is a former nurses' residence leased from the State. Its staff consists of an executive director, a program director, a secretary, two recent college graduates, and an ex-Peace Corpsman and an ex-offender who are both being trained in the skills of operating a community-based program. Also on staff are 12 to 15 male and female resident counselors, mostly college students.

PORT considers the students, in particular, as vital elements in the successful operation of the program:

> In effect they replace the guard/counselor
> staff of the institution. In return for
> board and room, they provide three primary
> functions: (1) They cover the building
> during off-duty hours in the capacity we
> call O.D.; (2) having been selected for
> their general competence and positive value
> system, they help develop and maintain a
> "healthy" culture in the program; and (3)
> along with the residents they maintain the
> building.[12]

Juvenile and district courts usually make the referrals to PORT, but entrance into the program is voluntary. Each candidate spends a three-week evaluation period in residence at PORT during which he and the screening committee determine whether they both feel he would benefit by participating in the program.

---

[11] Kenneth F. Schoen, "PORT: a new concept of community based correction," Federal Probation, September, 1972, p. 35.

[12] Ibid., pp. 35-36.

The core of the program consists not only of group treatment, but also of behavior modification. The behavior modification feature was added after the program had been in operation for a year, when the staff found that the groups alone were insufficient.

> Group sessions were spending too much time on an individual's problems in school and job performance, inconsistencies developed in ascertaining acceptable levels of performance, and the newcomer's association with groups of often varying value systems confused him. Also, the fact that the program was experiencing some failures led to the addition. A point system is used to mete out levels of freedom systematically, based upon measured performance in tangible areas. These include weekly school and work reports, building clean-up, managing a budget, planning and carrying out social activities successfully, and similar accomplishments.[13]

One of the keys to PORT's operation is the involvement of the community and the heavy use of its existing resources. PORT is actually run by a corporate board of directors, made up of members of the community; a group of 65 Rochester citizens, the PORT Advisory Committee, provides support in the areas of education, employment, social involvement, legislation, finance, and public awareness. Since PORT also relies on community resources such as public schools, mental health clinics, and sheltered workshops where supervised vocational work is provided, rather than maintaining its own facilities in these areas, the community's involvement is clearly essential to the program's successful operation.

While it is still too early to make a comprehensive evaluation of PORT, the program appears promising. In addition, some of the tentative

[13] Ibid., p. 36.

conclusions its advocates have drawn from it may be able to provide guidelines for future programs:

1. Mixing juveniles and adults in the community setting is not only practical, but preferred. The mature offender's impact on the delinquent's troublesome behavior is positive, and the youth's presence tends to make the older resident's immature performances look more outrageous.

2. College students, if they are carefully screened and supervised, can satisfactorily replace the custody or cottage staff.

3. Using existing local resources when possible allows the cottage to avoid the problems of developing separate special programs in such areas as vocational and academic training.

HALFWAY HOUSES

The halfway house concept covers more than one kind of facility. Originally, a halfway (out) house was a place for transition: It was a step between the prison and parole in the open community. In a halfway house an offender might learn how to get a job, rent a house, or become involved in group counseling. (The types of activities residents got involved in depended upon which programs were given priority by the house's director; accordingly, they varied greatly from one house to the next.)

Some of the best "halfway out" programs in the United States are the federal pre-release guidance centers. Each of these centers houses about 20 offenders, prisoners who have several months to go before their expected parole date.

Recently, however, the halfway house has begun to serve as an alternative to institutionalization and probation, rather than a pre-release center. This type of halfway house provides more constant, close supervision than probation can give, and is expected to replace imprisonment for

159

those who do not need to be in such an extremely restrictive setting.

INTENSIVE COMMUNITY TREATMENT

One of the most carefully planned and researched alternatives to imprisonment is the California Youth Authority's Community Treatment Program, established in 1961. According to some reports, the CTP has produced lower recidivism rates and improved psychological test scores compared to similar subjects in traditional Youth Authority institutional programs.[14] (James Robison and others, however, have indicated that, at least in the case of recidivism, the analysis of the CTP data may have been manipulated to make the success rate with the youths in the program appear more favorable.[15])

The youths in this program are boys and girls who initially have been screened in a reception center. During this screening process, youths who show a pattern of mental abnormality, have committed extremely serious crimes, or would arouse strenuous community objection to their direct release are eliminated from the group accepted for treatment in the CTP. (These exceptional youths may amount to 25% of the boys and 5-10% of the girls.) The youth admitted to the CTP is then classified in terms of his maturity, his perception of the world, the manner in which he interacts with his peers, and how he goes about meeting his needs. An interview and a number of standardized tests are used to

[14] M. Q. Warren, "The case for differential treatment of delinquents," The Annals of the American Academy of Political and Social Science, 381, January, 1969, pp. 47-59.

[15] James Robison and Gerald Smith, "The effectiveness of correctional programs," Crime and Delinquency, 17 (1), 1971, pp. 67-80.

accomplish this. Once the youth has been typed, he is intensively treated (ratio: 1 staff member to 12 youths) according to the plan that has been developed to meet the needs of the offender type he most closely approximates. The approaches used may include standard methods of treatment such as individual and group counseling, family therapy, group activities, and academic tutoring.

Since the CTP was well researched, and is being so professionally operated, its failures will have a great impact on advocates of community treatment for offenders. If an intensive community experiment such as this fails, correctional rehabilitators will have another cause for pessimism about the feasibility of community treatment in general.

PROBLEMS OF COMMUNITY TREATMENT

Community alternates to incarceration have not been established and operated without problems. Many of the significant difficulties these programs face can be traced back to a failure on the part of the project director to involve both the correctional and local communities in the program's operation.

The Pinehills project in Provo, Utah, described earlier in this chapter as an innovative Guided Group Interaction experiment, is no longer an active program. Though it appeared to have good possibilities as a community alternative to prison, it was functioning on a grant and was never incorporated into a correctional system to ensure it would continue.

The support of the local community is also needed if a community-based correctional project is to function effectively. As one correctional administrator notes, "To be merely tolerated by a community will not suffice. The genuine integration of the unit into the fabric of the community is necessary if our notion that the

161

community must be the context of treatment is to be anything more than a platitude."[16] One of the greatest difficulties encountered by all types of community-based corrections—halfway house, probation, parole—has been the distrust such programs seem to arouse in the average American community. In a recent survey by Harris Associates, a high proportion of respondents expressed a feeling of uneasiness working with a person who had been in prison for a violent crime. In general, such uneasiness and unfavorable attitude towards ex-offenders also correlated with low education and income.

To enlist community support for their programs, a number of project directors have attempted to involve local citizens in the initial planning stages, and provide them with information on the purpose and limits of community-based corrections. One of the points clarified in such early policy meetings is that while the center might accept offenders who have committed serious crimes, it would take all possible steps to avoid admitting dangerous offenders who should be institutionalized.

From the information now available on the success rates of traditional correctional institutions, it is fair to say that they have not been effective. However, in advocating community-based corrections as an alternative to imprisonment, one must be careful not to defend this approach more strenuously than it deserves at this point. Although it is not as costly as institutionalization and does not force the offender to break with his community and live in an abnormal—often destructive—setting, community treatment has still not proven itself to be <u>more</u> effective than imprisonment in a majority of experiments. Furthermore, the complete abolishment of prisons would be a naive, hasty action,

[16] H. B. Bradley, "Community-based treatment for young adult offenders," <u>Crime and Delinquency</u>, Vol. 15, No. 3, 1969, p. 360.

since some dangerous offenders do seem to require institutionalization. Norman Carlson, Director of the Federal Bureau of Prisons, described proposals to shut down prisons as a "desperate effort to find an overnight solution for some of the admitted failures of correctional institutions in the past."[17]

Yet, while the unlimited use of community programs in place of incarceration is not practical, the findings of at least one comprehensive study have indicated that the use of probation and community alternates to incarceration should be expanded, since a considerable number of offenders now incarcerated are no more dangerous than many of those already on probation.[18] Moreover, the assumption that sentencing more offenders to probation instead of prison would result in proportionally greater probation violations is also not supported by the available data.[19]

Limiting incarceration to dangerous offenders and channeling the bulk of other offenders to some form of community-based program or probation would seem, then, to provide inexpensive, humane treatment with at least as much likelihood of success as imprisonment. If the National Council on Crime and Delinquency's recommendation for a national moratorium on jail-building until all community alternatives have

[17] Remarks by Federal Bureau of Prisons Director Norman A. Carlson, made before a University of Miami corrections seminar, February, 1973.

[18] The California Assembly Office of Research, Preliminary Report on the Costs and Effects of the California Criminal Justice System and Recommendations for Legislation To Increase Support of Local Police and Corrections Programs, Sacramento, 1969.

[19] James Robison, The California Prison, Parole and Probation System, California Assembly Office of Research, 1969, pp. 27-32.

163

been developed is followed, the impact of community-based corrections on recidivism may be even more dramatic than is currently expected. Community-based treatment is not a cure-all, but in many cases it is one positive alternative that should definitely be tried.

CORE REFERENCES

President's Commission on Law Enforcement and Administration of Justice. Task Force Report: Corrections. Washington, D.C.: U.S. Government Printing Office, 1967.
    A Presidential Commission's report on special community-based techniques and an examination of the status of corrections in general.

Klapmuts, Nora. "Community Alternatives to Prison." Crime and Delinquency Literature, June, 1973, pp. 305-337.
    A recent, comprehensive article favoring the expanded use of community-based corrections in place of incarceration.

CHAPTER 10

Future of
Correctional Psychology

Correctional psychology's future depends on
whether it can show itself to be an effective
catalyst in the process of offender rehabilitation. We have discussed many of the ways correctional psychology has been, or could be, used to
improve traditional means of rehabilitation.
Some criminal justice officials recently have
expressed doubt, however, that psychologists
really can achieve such new and better results.

Judge David L. Bazelon, for example, in a
paper presented to the Lake Wales Conference in
Florida in 1972, called psychologists to task
for the ineffectualness of psychological intervention in corrections. He suggested that they
face their failures and take steps to initiate a
process of self-criticism and reexamination.

Psychologists have not produced any remark-
able successes in the corrections field.
But apparently that has never been a
sufficient reason to scrutinize your work
closely. After all, our entire correctional process is a shambles, and it is
hard to single out psychologists for blame
when none of the other participants has
been able to generate successful programs.

Moreover, psychology is still widely
considered a fledgling discipline in the
field of corrections, and it is often
assumed that it needs breathing room and
time to establish itself before it can make
inroads on the problem. Demanding quick
results could smother the effort, or encourage programs that sacrifice long-range
promise for short-term pay-offs. And
finally, even if we were prepared to hold
psychologists to a stringent standard of
accountability, we simply don't have any
uniformly agreed upon standard to measure
your performance. . . . No one on the
outside has been able to take psychology
on its own terms and ask whether it has
moved the ball forward or provided data
which would enable others to begin understanding our problems. Accordingly, if
any questioning is to be done, you are the
ones who must do it.

. . . I don't know whether psychology should
have a significant role, and I don't even
know how to find it except by asking you.
If you undertake the inquiry I am suggest-
ing, you may reach the painful conclusion
that you have completely misdirected your
efforts in trying to solve the problems of
crime and corrections. More likely, however, you will conclude that psychology
does have a limited role, but that its
potential abilities have been grossly over-
stated.[1]

The criticism of this eminent jurist is not
unreasonable; after all, the statement that psychology has not produced numerous successes in
the correctional field is accurate. In conceding

[1]Address by Judge David L. Bazelon of the U.S. Court
of Appeals, Washington, D.C., to the Lake Wales Conference, Florida, January, 1972.

that such a critical evaluation is valid, however, we must inquire why this has been the case, and how seriously it dampens the prospects for correctional psychology in the future.

Psychology has not borne impressive results in the past for quite a few reasons. Two of the major ones are (1) the continual rejection psychologists have met with from some correctional administrators, and (2) the inadequate training levels and insufficient number of psychologists on most prison staffs.

Even during this age of prison reform, the psychologist still is often considered an "outsider" by prison administrations. As a matter of fact, sometimes he is ignored, misused, or even abused by the director of the facility in which he is working. Unless the psychologist is allowed to take an active role as a member of an interdisciplinary team concerned with offender treatment, he cannot be expected to produce favorable results.

Another factor contributing to correctional psychology's image of failure is the type of representation the psychology profession has had in prison systems in the past. In many cases, either there have been too few psychologists, or the ones present were not adequately trained.

FUTURE OF CORRECTIONAL PSYCHOLOGY

It seems fair to say, then, that <u>correctional psychology has not been tried and found wanting; in the full sense, it has not really been tried yet</u>! Fortunately, the climate is changing now, and psychology soon should have greater opportunities to lend a positive hand in offender treatment. Today, a growing number of enlightened correctional administrators recognize that the psychologist must be included in correctional planning. In addition, psychology's professional associations are finally becoming more active in encouraging their members to apply themselves in the area of offender treatment. As a result, colleges and universities are beginning to offer special training in correctional psychology.

At the undergraduate level, courses in penology, criminology, and criminal justice are now giving added emphasis to the work being done by correctional psychologists. At the graduate level, the University of Alabama recently instituted a special major in correctional psychology, including M.A. and Ph.D. programs. Florida State, Southern Illinois, Middle Tennessee, and Chicago State are universities that also have extensive programs in either correctional psychology or correctional counseling. In the same vein, other universities are offering new internships at penal institutions for their clinical psychology students. One such program, which has served to introduce students to work in correctional facilities, was recently originated by Long Island University. This university established pre-internships and internships within the New York City Prison System, not only to train the students involved, but also to encourage them to enter the correctional field.

New roles are being opened up for correctional psychologists as well. In the past, psychologists often performed ill-conceived, inappropriate, ineffective functions. They were locked into limited traditional roles. Instead of serving the full prison population, psychologists spent endless hours doing individual therapy with isolated cases. Tomorrow's correctional psychologist no longer should be confined to a role based on a case model, where he operates only as a psychotherapist. Rather, as a member of an interdisciplinary team that might include a social worker, a psychiatrist, a correction officer, and other pertinent personnel, he should be able to help explore and contribute to the overall plans developed to treat the offender. Instead of acting simply as a practitioner, he could offer his services as trainer, researcher, and consultant.

Consequently, when psychology is given a real opportunity to take a more expanded, active role in the treatment of offenders, it will have a positive impact on corrections. And once psychology shows itself to be an effective catalyst in the offender rehabilitation process, future critics will no longer ask, "Should correctional psychology fill only a limited role?", but will demand to know, "What else can the correctional psychologist do within the penal system?" Correctional psychology's future possibilities are not limited; on the contrary, there seem to be no bounds to its full potential.

CORE REFERENCES

Brodsky, Stanley L. Psychologists in the Criminal Justice System. Carbondale, Illinois: American Association of Correctional Psychologists, 1972.
This report contains a complete description of what psychologists do in the criminal justice system, along with prospects for the future of correctional psychology.

APPENDIX

Reality therapy owes its popularity primarily to the work of
William Glasser. His practice, lectures, and writings on
this therapeutic approach have made him its chief spokesman.
In his book Reality Therapy, where he discusses its theory
and practice, the case of "Jeri" is particularly instructive.
"Patient responsibility" and "therapeutic involvement," two
of the concepts emphasized by reality therapists, are illus-
trated in this case.*

Jeri was referred to me because the record
stated that she was potentially suicidal. She was
in the discipline cottage, not because she had broken rules, but because she had said that she would
not go out into the school program. If we did not
put her in a room and leave her alone, she said she
would try to kill herself. In the discipline unit,
she cried a great deal, alternating the crying with
periods of hysterical laughter. She was intent on
creating the impression that she belonged in a mental hospital instead of Ventura. A psychiatrist is
usually asked to see girls like Jeri because the
staff feels uncomfortable without some special guidance. About a week before, I had seen her briefly
for an initial interview during which she said that
she wanted no part of the school and would not cooperate in the program. Having heard this many times
before from girls who had just arrived, I did not
take it seriously. Evidently she had meant what
she said, for she had succeeded in getting herself
removed from the program and in worrying the staff
about her sanity.

Jeri was a short, attractive, intelligent
sixteen-year-old girl who had caused so much conflict in her home in Florida that her parents had
sent her to an uncle in San Francisco. Shortly
after arriving in San Francisco, she ran away
from her uncle and, for the eighteen months before
coming to Ventura, had supported herself in the
San Francisco area by shoplifting. Living with a

*Excerpts from pp. 75-80 in Reality Therapy by William
Glasser, M.D. Copyright © 1965 by William Glasser, M.D.
Reprinted by permission of Harper & Row, Publishers, Inc.

group of older girls and women who stole for their
support, she was involved in criminal activities
as much as any of her older companions or even
more than they. She posed as nineteen, refused
to admit her true age, and boasted that at least
one large department store in San Francisco must
be out of the red now that she was locked up.
Many of the things she stole she had no use for;
much was wasted, thrown away, or given away. The
act of stealing expensive furs, for example, was
more important than the furs themselves.

Jeri was committed to the California Youth
Authority because she was caught stealing an
inexpensive blouse from a Southern California
store on an infrequent trip south. She complained
bitterly that she should have just been put in
jail for ten days as an adult instead of having
to go to the California Youth Authority. It was
like slipping on a banana peel after successfully
shooting Niagara Falls.

In our initial conversation I said I wanted
to help her get out of Ventura and stay out of
trouble, but I could not do anything for her
unless she would consent to leave her room in the
discipline cottage. Although agreeing that she
was upset, I told her I believed she felt upset
mainly because she had been caught. I refused to
discuss her threat of suicide, and when she
brought it up I told her what I usually tell girls
who threaten to take their lives, "We can't help
you if you kill yourself. We have no program for
girls who threaten suicide, and there is abso-
lutely no chance of your being transferred to a
mental hospital." (Very few girls are transferred
to mental hospitals because generally we have much
better facilities for treating girls with any kind
of irresponsibility, including psychosis.) Adding
that she was welcome to spend as much time as she
wished in her room in the discipline cottage, I
noted that the time spent there would be of no use
in helping her. I repeated I would like to help
her, that we had a good program, and that we
wanted her to give it a chance. This part of the
conversation was blended into a friendly get-

acquainted discussion of our school, our program, of me and my work, and of her life over the past few months. Although I did not agree with her method, I did respect her attempt to assert herself, and I intimated that the same effort in a different direction might do her much more good.

When I left, we were on good terms. She promised nothing and I did not push her for a decision about leaving the discipline cottage. I told her, however, that this was the last time I would see her there although I would be happy to see her in my office if she changed her mind. Altogether it was a pleasant interview in which I was completely honest and serious with her. I wrote a note telling the staff to pay no attention to her desire to be recognized as mentally ill, not to worry that she would commit suicide, and to leave her alone to think over what I had said.

Three days later when I came back to the school there was a note from Jeri saying that she had decided "to give up acting crazy," that she had entered the school program, and that she wanted to see me in my office. When she came she made light of what she had done in the discipline cottage and put on a determined effort to be friendly and ingratiating. Saying she had come into the program as a favor to me, she wanted to know how soon I was going to get her out. I said that when she was released depended upon how she acted in the program, adding that I would be glad to see her regularly once a week for half an hour. Because at that time I did not have a group to place her in and because I had not seen a patient individually for a long while, I decided to do so for a change, although it is not my regular practice at Ventura.

At best, she behaved only adequately in the program. Our conversations were mostly friendly arguments in which she concentrated on what I could do for her and how "we" would work to get her out. Telling her that it was up to her and not me, I tried with little success to break

through her shell to find some interest. Instead,
she discussed how she would go back to stealing.

All during therapy and especially toward the
time that she would ordinarily have been considered ready for parole, I pointed out to her that
she had little feeling for anyone in the world
except herself. I told her that as much as I
enjoyed talking to her and as well as she seemed
to be doing at times in the kitchen program,
unless she began to consider the rights and
feelings of other people, both here at the school
and in the community, she would go right back to
being a thief when she left. I always emphasized
the word thief, never glossing over the offense
with the milder euphemism, shoplifter. At the
same time I heard that in the cottage she did
everything possible to avoid work while still
looking as if she was busy.

When the time came for referral to parole,
the big moment at Ventura, the housemother did
not think that she had sincerely tried to work
into the program, and she was especially influ-
enced to refuse to recommend her when Jeri said,
"You have to refer me because Dr. Glasser thinks
I'm doing good." I had already told the housemother to hold her if she did not feel she was
ready, and Jeri was really shaken when her time
at the school was extended a month. She threatened to go back to her old "crazy" behavior. She
cried, she disparaged her housemother, she claimed
I broke my promises, said I had no real influence,
and that the school was unfair.

During the next month she did not do well.
As much as she complained of my inadequacy to my
face, she began to spread rumors that she was
"in" with me, and that I would do anything for
her. Part of this behavior is natural for a girl
who is getting involved with a person who has
some status, a kind of namedropping, but when it
continues as it did here, it becomes a way for
her to escape from responsibility. It was necessary to confront her with what she was doing. The
climax came after I warned her several times

174

about saying that I was doing favors for her.
Despite her bland denials, I heard from several
sources, staff and other girls, that she had said
I had mailed letters for her, a serious violation
of our strict rule about censoring mail.

When I definitely confirmed that she had
said it, I went to her cottage and told her that
she would have to go to the discipline unit. As
difficult as it is to confront and discipline a
girl who is in therapy, I had no choice. Knowing how uncomfortable it made me, she played my
discomfort for all it was worth. She put on an
emotional scene in front of all the girls in the
cottage, stating that my charges were all lies,
that I only wanted to lock her up to keep her
from leaving, that my attempt to help her was
phony, and that she never wanted to see me again.
I listened, restated that I wanted to help her,
and told her I would see her next at our regular
time in the discipline cottage. She walked away
crying and saying that I could not be her friend
or help her any more. She made it sound as if I
had committed the unpardonable sin by confronting her with the reality of her behavior.
Actually, she was testing my intentions, trying
to find out whether I really did care what she
did and what she said, whether I could stand up
to her attempt to downgrade me in front of the
other girls, and whether I would show retali-
atory anger. Girls are willing to accept discipline but not punishment; they differentiate
between the two by seeing whether the disciplin-
ing person shows anger and gets satisfaction by
exercising power. What followed worked only
because I neither felt nor showed that I was
punishing her.

The following week when I went to the
discipline unit Jeri was anxious to see me. As
soon as she came into the office it was apparent
that our involvement had been strengthened. My
standing firm and rejecting her, as evidenced by
my continued interest in seeing her after all
that she had said about me, had broken through.

Appendix

    She was greatly changed. She asked me how
long she would have to stay in the discipline
cottage. Saying that I would leave it up to her
to tell me when she was ready to leave, I helped
her by adding that she could prepare for leaving
by telling the truth and changing some of her
ways. She then poured out the story of her
deceitful life, her lies and misbehavior at the
school, and how worried she was about her future.
Instead of forgiving her, which used to be my
natural impulse before I discovered how wrong it
is therapeutically, I told her she was right to
feel miserable and probably would continue to
feel bad for the next few weeks. When I left I
told her I would see her next week. Her desire
to stay in discipline was therapeutic—knowing
that she had thinking to do and feelings of guilt
to overcome, she realized that the discipline
cottage was the best place for her.

    In Reality Therapy it is important not to
minimize guilt when it is deserved, and Jeri
deserved to feel as bad as she did. Although she
felt better the next week, she still did not think
she was ready to leave the discipline unit. We
talked mostly of her future and how she would have
to take care of herself. Not wanting to go back
to Florida to her family, she requested that she
be paroled to a foster home in San Diego, which we
arranged. The following week, after three weeks
in discipline, she was ready to return to her
cottage. The remainder of the time in therapy was
spent planning in detail what she would do when
she was released, especially how she would avoid
old friends and old temptations. She left after
eight months, three and a half months more than
our minimum program. Everyone noticed how much
she had changed, particularly her housemother,
whom she now loved—a great contrast with earlier
times when she had told me how hateful and prejudiced her housemother was.

    In summary, we could see that when Jeri
tested me to find out whether I really cared,
there was enough involvement for me to pass the
test in her eyes by placing her in discipline.

176

If I had not done so she would never have changed;
if we had not been moderately involved it would
not have worked. When I rejected her irresponsibility but maintained interest in her, our involvement solidified, and she then began to fulfill her
needs. The rest of therapy was relearning, mainly
detailed planning for her future.

GENERAL BIBLIOGRAPHY

Ackerman, John R. "Reality therapy approach to probation and parole supervision." Probation and Parole, 1(1):15-17, 1969.

Acquilano, John N. "The Monroe County Pilot Probation Program: a preliminary report." Probation and Parole (New York), n.v.(3): 74-75, 1971.

Adams, Leon Reed. An experimental evaluation of the adequacy of differential association theory and a theoretical formulation of a learning theory of criminal behavior. (Dissertation) Ann Arbor, Mich.: University Microfilms, 1972. 222 pages.

Adams, Stuart. College-level instruction in U.S. prisons: an exploratory survey. Berkeley: University of California, School of Criminology, 1968. 46 pages.

Adams, Stuart. "Education and the career dilemma of high IQ prisoners." Criminologica, 6(4): 4-12, 1969.

Adams, Stuart. The San Quentin Prison College Project: final report, phase 1. Berkeley: University of California, School of Criminology, 1968. 79 pages.

Adams, Stuart, and Connolly, John J. "Role of junior colleges in the prison community." Junior College Journal, March:92-98, 1971.

Adams, William T., Grant, Richard A., and Prigmore, Charles S. "Relationship of correctional to vocational rehabilitation." Crime and Delinquency, 12(3):227-231, 1966.

Akman, Dogan D. "Homicide and assaults in Canadian penitentiaries." Howard Journal of Penology and Crime Prevention, 12(2):102- 112, 1967.

General Bibliography

Akman, Dogan D., Normandeau, Andre, and Wolfgang, Marvin E. "The group treatment literature in correctional institutions: an international bibliography, 1945-1967." Journal of Criminal Law, Criminology and Police Science, 59(1):41-56, 1968.

Alachua County Sheriff's Office, Inmate and Community Services Project. Establishing helping services in local jails. Florida, 1971. 56 pages.

Alaimo, Charles. "A group program in retrospect." Youth Service News, 20(3):15-16, 34, 1969.

Allen, James E. "The silent observer: a new approach to group therapy for delinquents." Crime and Delinquency, 16(3):324-328, 1970.

Allen, Thomas E. "Patterns of escape and self-destructive behavior in a correctional institution." Corrective Psychiatry and Journal of Social Therapy, 15(2):50-58, 1969.

Alper, Benedict S. "The training school: step-child of public education." Federal Probation (Washington, D.C.), 33(4):24-28, 1969.

American Correctional Association. Manual of correctional standards. Washington, D.C.: American Correctional Association, 1959. See particularly "Recreation," pp. 519-540.

American Correctional Association. Proceedings of the 95th annual Congress of Correction. Washington, D.C., 1965. 296 pages.

American Correctional Association. Proceedings of the 97th annual Congress of Correction. Washington, D.C., 1967. 338 pages.

American Correctional Association. Proceedings of the 98th annual Congress of Correction. Washington, D.C., 1969. 354 pages.

American Correctional Association. <u>Proceedings of the 99th annual Congress of Correction</u>. Washington, D.C., 1970. 362 pages.

American Correctional Association. <u>Proceedings of the 100th annual Congress of Correction</u>. College Park, Md., 1971. 402 pages.

American Correction Association. <u>Riots and Disturbances</u>. Washington, D.C.: ACA, 1970.

Anderson, Kent. "College anyone?" <u>Presidio</u>, 33(5):16, 37, 1966.

Andrews, Frank Earl, and Dickens, Albert, eds. <u>Voices from the Big House</u>. Detroit: Harlo Press, 1972. 190 pages.

Arnold, William R., and Stiles, Bill. "A summary of increasing use of 'group methods' in correctional institutions." <u>International Journal of Group Psychotherapy</u>, 22(1):77-92, 1972.

Association for the Psychiatric Treatment of Offenders. <u>New York APTO Therapists' report</u>. <u>International Journal of Offender Therapy</u> (London), 1970. 39 pages. (Offender Therapy Series, APTO Monographs No. 2)

Association of State Correction Administrators. <u>Policy guidelines: health services, disciplinary procedures, classification and assignment of inmates, access to media, racial issues, mail, exercise and recreation, and visiting</u>. Columbia, S.C., 1972.

Atlas, Thomas A. "An analytical survey of the use of group counseling in correctional institutions." <u>Probation and Parole</u>, n.v. (3):13-26, 1971.

Attrill, Gerry. "Drama as an evening activity." <u>Community Schools Gazette</u> (Dartford, England), 64(9):509-512, 1970.

General Bibliography

Avery, C. L.   "Industrial training at San Quentin."
    Correctional Review, n.v. (May/June):2-6,
    1967.

Ayllon, Teodoro, Layman, Dale, and Burke, Sandra.
    "Disruptive behavior and reinforcement of
    academic performance." Psychological Record
    (Granville, Ohio), 22(3):315-323, 1972.

Baden, Michael M.   "Homicide, suicide, and acci-
    dental death among narcotic addicts." Human
    Pathology, vol. 3, no. 1, March 1972.

Baker, Jerry. "They must be educated."
    Journal of Correctional Education, 17(3):
    19-22, 1965.

Balogh, Joseph K.   "Conjugal visitation in
    prisons: a sociological perspective."
    Federal Probation, vol. 28, 1964.

Baril, F. W.   "Vocational training in Canadian
    penitentiaries." Journal of Correctional
    Education, 19(2):16-17, 27, 28, 1967.

Barker, E. T., and Mason, M. H.   "The insane
    criminal as therapist." Canadian Journal of
    Corrections, 10(4):553-561, 1968.

Barrett, Donald R.   "A study of academic perform-
    ance in correctional education." Journal of
    Correctional Education, 16(4):13-16, 1964.

Bates, Gerald K.   "Prison TV for education."
    American Journal of Correction, 29(1):20-22,
    1967.

Belcastro, Frank P.   "The use of programmed
    instruction in Canadian correctional institu-
    tions." Canadian Journal of Corrections,
    11(4):233-239, 1969.

Belcastro, Frank P., Cocha, Walter A., and
    Valois, A. John.   "The use of programmed
    instruction in United States correctional
    institutions." Journal of Correctional

Education (Menard, Ill.), 22(1):14-17, 42,
1970.

Beless, Donald W., and Pilcher, William S.
Probation officer—case aide project: a
summary progress report. Chicago: University of Chicago, Center for Studies in
Criminal Justice, 1969. 27 pages.

Beless, Donald W., Pilcher, William S., and Ryan,
Ellen Jo. "Use of indigenous nonprofession-
als in probation and parole." Federal
Probation, 36(1):10-15, 1972.

Belle, Oslen S. "Social reinforcement of deviant
and pathological behavior." Canadian Journal
of Corrections, 11(4):262-270, 1969.

Beresford, Robert. "Group therapy for chronic
violators." Trial, 7(2):42, 1971.

Bernath, L. L. "The techniques of motivation in
correctional institutions." Journal of
Correctional Education, 17(1):6-11, 1965.

Berne, Eric. Games People Play. New York: Grove
Press, 1964.

Berne, Eric. Principles of Group Treatment. New
York: Oxford University Press, 1966.

Berne, Eric. Transactional Analysis in Psychotherapy. New York: Grove Press, 1961.

Beto, Dan Richard, and Claghorn, James L.
"Factors associated with self-mutilation
within the Texas Department of Corrections."
American Journal of Correction, 30(1):25-27,
1968.

Blank, Lucile E. "Education in a short-term
institution." American Journal of Correction, 28(6):21-23, 1966.

Bluestone, Harvey, O'Malley, Edward P., and
    Connell, Sydney. "Homosexuals in prison."
    Corrective Psychiatry and Journal of Social
    Therapy, vol. 12, no. 1, 1966.

Blum, Gerald S. Psychoanalytic Theories of
    Personality. New York: McGraw-Hill, 1953.

Boschi, Filippo. "Il concetto di 'propedeutica'
    nell addestramento professionale die minori
    disadattati." (The concept of "initiation"
    in the vocational training of maladjusted
    minors.) Esperienze di Rieducasione, 14(5):
    18-36, 1967.

Bowers, Richard A. "Public schools lend a hand."
    Youth Authority Quarterly (Sacramento,
    Calif.), 23(8):25-30, 1970.

Bradley, H. B. "Community-based treatment for
    young adult offenders." Crime and Delin-
    quency, vol. 15, no. 3, 1969.

Bratter, Thomas Edward. "Treating adolescent
    drug abusers in a community-based inter-
    action group program: some philosophical
    considerations." Journal of Drug Issues,
    1(3):237-252, 1971.

Breeskin, John. "The airmen's readjustment group
    therapy program." Corrective Psychiatry and
    Journal of Social Therapy, 16(1, 2, 3, & 4):
    103-113, 1970.

Brodsky, Stanley L. "Prisoner evaluations of
    correctional programs," in Brodsky,
    Stanley L., and Eggleston, Norman E., eds.,
    The Military Prison. Carbondale: Southern
    Illinois University Press, 1970, pp. 152-258.

Brodsky, Stanley L. Psychologists in the Criminal
    Justice System. Carbondale, Illinois:
    American Association of Correctional Psychol-
    ogists, 1972.

Brooks, Ernest C. "Something new in prison responsibility." American Journal of Correction, 27(1):14-16, 1965.

Buckley, Marie. "Enter: the ex-con." Federal Probation, 36(4), December, 1972.

Buehler, R. E., Patterson, G. R., and Furniss, J. M. "The reinforcement of behavior in institutional settings." Behavioral Research and Therapy, 4(3):157-167, 1966.

Buffum, Peter C. Homosexuality in Prisons. Washington, D.C.: U.S. Dept. of Justice, LEAA, National Institute of Law Enforcement and Criminal Justice, 1972.

Burchard, J. D., and Tyler, V. O., Jr. The modification of delinquent behavior through operant conditioning. Paper read at the American Pathological Association meeting, 1964.

Burke, Allen E. "Vocational orientation." Journal of Correctional Education, 20(1): 19-20, 1968.

Byrd, Robert C. "Education will be the key to rehabilitation." American Journal of Correction, 29(2):4-6, 1967.

California Corrections Department. Vocational training at the California Institution for Women: an evaluation, by Carol Spencer and John E. Berecochea. Sacramento, 1971. 33 pages.

California State Assembly. Report on the economic status and rehabilitation value of California correctional industries. Sacramento, 1969. 68 pages.

California Youth Authority Department. A four-year report: 1965-1968. Sacramento, 1969. 32 pages.

General Bibliography

California Youth Authority Department. Education course descriptions. Sacramento, 1970. 155 pages.

California Youth Authority Department. Compensatory Education in the California Youth Authority, 1968-1969. Sacramento, 1970. 38 pages.

California Youth Authority Department. Compensatory education in the California Youth Authority, 1969-1970. Sacramento, 1970. 32 pages.

California Youth Authority Department. Interim assessment of the Jobs Related to Training Project, by Joachim P. Seckel. Sacramento, 1970. 19 pages.

California Youth Authority Department. Progress report on the differential education project—Paso Robles School for Boys, by Jo Ann Mahan and Carl R. Andre. January, 1971. 12 pages. (Educational Research Series Report No. 2)

California Youth Authority Department. The Los Angeles Community Delinquency Control Project: an experiment in the rehabilitation of delinquents in an urban community. Los Angeles, 1970. 51 pages.

California Youth Authority Department. The Marshall Program—assessment of a short-term institutional treatment program. Part I: Parole outcome and background characteristics, by Doug Knight. Sacramento, 1969. 88 pages. (Research Report No. 56)

California Youth Authority Department. The Marshall Program: assessment of a short-term institutional treatment program. Part II: Amenability to confrontive peer-group treatment, by Doug Knight. Sacramento, 1970. (Research Report No. 59)

Campbell, Jay, and Clannon, Thomas L. "From the Medical Facility of the California Department of Correction. Questionnaire-study of the aspects considered relevant by its group therapists." International Journal of Offender Therapy, 13(3):158-164, 1969.

Camper, John. "The teacher in the correctional school classroom." Youth Authority Quarterly, 17 (4):23-27, 1964.

Campos, Leonard P. "Developing eight 'therapeutic communities' at a school for boys." Youth Authority Quarterly, 20(2):20-31, 1967.

Catalino, Anthony. "Guided group interaction in Florida." Delinquency Prevention Report, June-July, 1971, pp. 3-8.

Catalino, Anthony. "Juvenile delinquents do strange things—like other people." American Journal of Correction (St. Paul), 33(1): 22-26, 1971.

Carpenter, Ruth Sarah. "An experiment in success-ful living." Youth Authority Quarterly, 19(4):9-14, 1966.

Carter, Robert D., and Stuart, Richard B. "Behavior modification theory and practice: a reply." Social Work, 15(1):37-50, 1970.

Case, John D. "Incentives in a county prison." Prison Journal, 47(1):4-11, 1967.

Cavan, Ruth Shonle. Criminology. New York: Thomas Y. Crowell, 1962.

Cavan, Ruth S., and Zemans, Eugene S. "Marital relationship of prisoners in twenty-eight countries." Journal of Criminal Law, Criminology and Police Science, July-August, vol. 49, no. 2, 1958.

General Bibliography

Chenault, Price. "Correctional institution
    helping the functionally illiterate." ALA
    Bulletin, 58(9):804-809, 1964.

Chopra, Pran. "Punishment and the control of
    human behavior." Australian and New Zealand
    Journal of Criminology, 2(3):149-157, 1969.

Claghorn, James L., and Beto, Dan Richard. "Self-
    mutilation in a prison mental hospital."
    Corrective Psychiatry and Journal of Social
    Therapy, 13(3):133-141, 1967.

Clayton, Tom. Men in Prison. London: Hamish
    Hamilton, 1970.

Clear, Val. Summer probation internship program
    1971 (final report). Anderson, Ind.:
    Anderson College, 1971. 42 pages.

Clemmer, Donald. "Some aspects of sexual
    behavior in the prison community."
    Proceedings of the American Correctional
    Association, Washington, D.C., 1958.

Codd, James E. "History of a functional voca-
    tional program." Proceedings of the American
    Correctional Association, Washington, D.C.,
    1963, pp. 130-133.

Coleman, Benjamin I. "Reality therapy with
    offenders: practice." International Journal
    of Offender Therapy, 14(1):26-31, 1970.

"College behind bars." Communications for
    Business, n.v. (Winter):2-7, 1972.

Conte, William R. "Correctional education—a
    many-faceted thing." Journal of Correctional
    Education, 19(4):10-11, 30, 1967.

Cooper, H. H. A. "Self-mutilation by Peruvian
    prisoners." International Journal of
    Offender Therapy (London), 15(3):180-188,
    1971.

Cormier, Bruno M. "Therapeutic community in a prison setting." International Annals of Criminology, 9(2):419-441, 1970.

Correctional Education Association & Southern Illinois University, Center for the Study of Crime, Delinquency, and Corrections. Papers and reports of the 14th annual Correctional Education Conference, June 7-9, 1965. Carbondale, Ill., 1965. 146 pages.

Correctional Service of Minnesota, Research Division. Volunteer groups in Minnesota criminal justice agencies. Minneapolis, 1971. 49 pages.

Council of Research and Evaluation. The USDB vocational follow-up study: final report, by John D. Nichols and Stanley L. Brodsky. Fort Leavenworth, Kansas, United States Disciplinary Barracks, no date. 6 pages.

Council on Social Work Education. The socio-behavioral approach and applications to social work, ed. by Edwin J. Thomas. New York, 1967. 100 pages.

Cox, Mary Louise. Report of experimental community relations program in Westchester County (N.Y.) Penitentiary. Chappaqua, N.Y., 1969. 6 pages.

Crabtree, Loren H., and Fox, James J. D. "The overthrow of a therapeutic community." International Journal of Group Psychotherapy, XXII (1), 1972.

Craig, Wayne O., and Gordon, George K. "Programmed instruction, teaching machines, and adult education." Journal of Correctional Education, 19(4):16-22, 1967.

Creane, John. "Young offenders at the crossroads." Manpower, September:24-28, 1969.

Cressey, Donald R., ed. The Prison: Studies in
    Institutional Organization and Change. New
    York: Holt, Rinehart & Winston, 1961.

Cross, Tim. College-in-prison. Feasibility
    study. Cambridge: Harvard University
    Press, 1969. 81 pages.

Curtin, John C. A captive audience: some sugges-
    tions for the prison college. School of
    Criminology, University of California at
    Berkeley, 1967. (unpublished)

Czajkoski, Eugene H. "The new wave of therapy
    in corrections." American Journal of
    Correction, 30(1):17-18, 1968.

Dahlgren, Arnold W., and Schlotterback, Darrell.
    "Educational opportunities in the United
    States disciplinary barracks." Journal of
    Correctional Education, 17(1):20-23, 1965.

Davis, Alan J. "Sexual assaults in the Philadel-
    phia prison system and sheriff's vans."
    Trans-action, 6(2):8-16, 1968.

Davis, I. Lorraine, and Kaminski, Katherine B.
    The use of groups at a training school for
    delinquent girls. An Occasional Paper of
    the School for Social Work (No. 6), Madison,
    University of Wisconsin, 1968, pp. 1-8.

Davis, William S. "Quality schools within insti-
    tutional settings." Journal of Correctional
    Education, 17(2):18-21, 1965.

Day, Peter R. "Aspects of learning and probation
    treatment." Probation (London), 18(1):13-17,
    1972.

Day, Sherman R., and Megathlin, William L. "Human
    relations program for nonprofessional person-
    nel in the correctional setting." Georgia
    Journal of Corrections, 1(2):72-78, 1972.

Denfeld, D. The role of student volunteers in corrections today. Storrs: University of Connecticut, 1971. 9 pages. (dittoed)

Dickover, Robert M., Maynard, Verner E., and Painter, James A. Five articles on vocational trainees in A study of vocational training in the California Department of Corrections. Sacramento: California Corrections Dept., 1971. (Research Report No. 40)

Dickover, Robert M., Maynard, Verner E., and Painter, James A. "The parole agent and the vocational trainee," in California Corrections Dept., The parole agent and the vocational trainee. Sacramento, 1971, pp. 77-88.

Didato, Salvatore U. "Delinquents in group therapy: some new techniques." Adolescence, 5(18):207-223, 1970.

Dingess, Leslie. "The function of vocational education in the total correctional process." Journal of Correctional Education, 17(2): 12-14, 1965.

District of Columbia Corrections Department. Disciplinary offenses and disciplinary offenders under two correctional climates, by Barry S. Brown and John D. Spevacek. Washington, D.C., 1969. 21 pages. (Research Report No. 17)

District of Columbia Corrections Department. Effectiveness of the Lorton Prison College Project: third interim report. Washington, D.C., 1972. 11 pages. (Research Memorandum 72-4)

District of Columbia Corrections Department. The D.C. prison college projects: an interim report, by Stuart Adams. Washington, D.C., 1970. 25 pages. (Research Report No. 28)

191

District of Columbia Corrections Department. The
    D.C. prison college projects: second year
    report. Washington, D.C., 1971.

District of Columbia Corrections Department. The
    educational program of the D.C. jail:
    analysis and recommendations, by Ann Jacobs,
    Stuart Adams, and Bernd Schulz. Washington,
    D.C., 1971. 35 pages. (Research Report
    No. 38)

Doleschal, Eugene. "Higher education in U.S.
    prisons." Information Review on Crime and
    Delinquency, vol. 1, no. 1, 1968.

Dorney, W. Patrick. "The educational program as
    part of a detention service." Federal
    Probation, 28(4):55-57, 1964.

Draper Correctional Center. The Draper experi-
    ment: a dramatic use of programmed instruc-
    tion in a prison for youthful offenders, by
    John M. McKee and Donna M. Seay. Paper
    presented at the Conference on Programmed
    Learning and Electronic Media in Educational
    and Training Systems of the Detroit Society
    for Programmed Instruction, January 28, 1965.
    Elmore, Alabama. 8 pages.

Dressler, David. Practice and theory of probation
    and parole. New York: Columbia University
    Press, 1969. 347 pages.

Durig, K. Robert. The group counseling project in
    Clark County, Indiana. Clark County, Ind.,
    no date. 46 pages.

Eckenrode, C. J. "Education's contributions to
    institutional treatment modules." Journal of
    Correctional Education, 21(2):5-8, 1969.

Eckenrode, C. J. "Meshing training and production
    gears in correctional institutions." Journal
    of Correctional Education, 16(1) and 16(2),
    1964.

Eckenrode, C. J. "Overview of the education department mission." Journal of Correctional Education, 17(4):20-22, 1965.

Eckenrode, C. J. "What makes correctional education correctional?" Journal of Correctional Education, 17(2):6-9, 1965.

Eftihiades, Theodore D., and Fink, Ludwig. "Study regarding the value of psychotherapy in prison." International Annals of Criminology, 7(1):9-14, 1968.

Elias, Albert. "Group treatment program for juvenile delinquents." Child Welfare, 47(5): 281-290, 1968.

Empey, LaMar T., and Newland, George E. "Staff-Inmate collaboration: a study of critical incidents and consequences in the Silverlake experiment." Journal of Research in Crime and Delinquency, 5(1), 1968.

Engel, S. W. "Therapy with offenders against property in Germany." International Journal of Offender Therapy, 13(1):21-26, 1969.

Engelbarts, Rudolf. Books in stir: a bibliographic essay about prison libraries and about books written by prisoners and prison employees. Metuchen, N.J.: Scarecrow Press, 1972. 168 pages.

Erwin, John R. "Cook County Jail's short-term education program." American Journal of Correction (St. Paul, Minn.), 32(2):14-18, 1970.

Eyman, Joy S. Prisons for women. Springfield, Ill.: Charles C. Thomas, 1971. 185 pages.

Fabian, Felix. "The role of colleges and universities in supporting the professionalization of correctional education." Journal of Correctional Education, 17(1):15-16, 1965.

General Bibliography

Feldman, Wulff. "Group counseling in Danish
    prisons." Police, 15(1):40-44, 1970.

Fenton, Norman, Reimer, Ernest G., and Wilmer,
    Harry A., eds. The correctional community:
    an introduction and guide. Berkeley:
    University of California Press, 1967. 119
    pages.

Ferstman, Abraham, and Williams, Paul J. "The
    training of personnel in a therapeutic
    community," in Quebec Society of Criminology,
    Proceedings: 5th Research Conference on
    Delinquency and Criminality. Montreal:
    Centre de Psychologie et de Pedagogie, 1967,
    pp. 161-168.

Fink, Ludwig, et al. "Clinton Project." Canadian
    Journal of Corrections, 10(2):321-326, 1968.

Fish, Lillian V. "New trends in vocational
    training, IBM project at Westfield State
    Farm." Journal of Correctional Education,
    18(1):15-18, 1966.

Fisher, Robert G. "The legacy of Freud—a dilemma
    for handling offenders in general and sex
    offenders in particular." University of
    Colorado Law Review, 40(2):242-267, 1968.

Fishman, Joseph. Sex in Prison. New York:
    National Library Press, 1934.

Florida's School for Boys at Okeechobee. Faculty
    self-analysis of educational programs.
    Okeechobee, Florida, 1969. 67 pages.

Florida Youth Services Division. Group program
    procedures at Florida's training schools.
    1971. 27 pages.

Flynn, Frank T. "Behind prison riots." Social
    Service Review, vol. 27, 1953.

194

Foley, Thomas J., Jr. "The efficiency of group psychotherapy with first-term airmen at an Air Force Technical Training Center." Corrective Psychiatry and Journal of Social Therapy, 16(1, 2, 3, & 4):46-50, 1970.

Forthun, Gerald J., and Nuehring, Ronald. Group work in a maximum security prison. An Occasional Paper of the School of Social Work (No. 6). Madison: University of Wisconsin, 1968.

Fox, Vernon. Introduction to Corrections. Englewood Cliffs, N.J.: Prentice-Hall, 1972.

Franks, Cyril M., ed. Behavior Therapy: Appraisal and Status. New York: McGraw-Hill, 1969.

Freedman, Marcia, and Pappas, Nick. The training and employment of offenders. Submitted to the President's Commission on Law Enforcement and Administration of Justice, Washington, D.C., 1967. 63 pages.

Freese, Amorette Lee. "Group therapy with exhibitionists and voyeurs." Social Work, 17(2):44-52, 1972.

Gartner, Alan. Paraprofessionals and their performance: a survey of education, health, and social service programs. New York: Praeger, 1971. 152 pages.

Georgia Education Department. Atlanta federal offenders rehabilitation project: final report, by W. Scott Fulton, 1970. 39 pages.

Georgia Institute of Government, Corrections Division. Behavior therapy: a guide to correctional administration and programming. Athens: University of Georgia, 1971. 67 pages.

General Bibliography

Gerdes, Ed.   "Ex-inmates can go to college."
     Presidio, 33(2):10-12, 33, 1966.

Gibbons, Don C.   "Violence in American society:
     the challenge to corrections." American
     Journal of Correction, 31(2):6-11, 1969.

Gilbert, G. M.   Personality Dynamics: A Biosocial
     Approach. New York: Harper & Row, 1970.

Gillooly, William B.   "A revolution in reading
     instruction at the training school." American
     Journal of Correction, 27(2):30-31, 1965.

Gilman, Merritt, and Gorlich, Elizabeth. Group
     counseling with delinquent youth. Children's
     Bureau publication No. 459, Washington, D.C.,
     1968.   38 pages.

Glaser, Daniel.   "Incentives for the alteration of
     offender behavior," in University of Alberta,
     The prevention of crime in medium-sized
     cities: some innovations in correctional
     practice. Banff: University of Alberta,
     1968, pp. 14-19.

Glaser, Daniel.   "Incentives motivating prisoner
     behavior." Prison Journal, 47(1):12-20,
     1967.

Glaser, Daniel.   "The effectiveness of correction-
     al education." American Journal of
     Correction, 28(2):4-9, 1966.

Glaser, Daniel.   "Work for prisoners" (Chapter II),
     in The effectiveness of a prison and parole
     system. Indianapolis, Ind.: Bobbs-Merrill,
     1965, pp. 224-259.

Glasser, William. Reality Therapy. New York:
     Harper & Row, 1965.

Glecker, Ronald A.   "Why education in prisons?"
     Journal of Correctional Education, 17(3):13,
     1965.

Gordon, John J. "The Pennsylvania public offender program of the Pennsylvania Bureau of Vocational Rehabilitation." Prison Journal, 47 (1):39-42, 1967.

Gorlich, Elizabeth H. "Group methods in institutional programming." Federal Probation, 32(4):46-49, 1968.

Guarriello, Ovidio, and Brunetti, Guido. "Le 'botteghe' di tempo libero e il lavoro-gioco." (Free-time shops and work-play.) Esperienze di Rieducazione, 14(9):5-18, 1967.

Gunn, Alex M. "Minority culture training in Youth Authority institutions." Youth Authority Quarterly, 22(2):13-17, 1969.

Hahn, Nicolas. "How to teach a delinquent." Atlantic, 223(3):66-72, 1969.

Hall, Donald S. "Education treatment center program." Youth Authority Quarterly (Sacramento, Calif.), 25(2):40-48, 1972.

Hall, Reis H. A study of post-release work experience of federal reformatory vocational trainees. Petersburg, Va.: Federal Reformatory, 1963. 11 pages.

Halleck, Seymour L., and Bromberg, Walter. Psychiatric aspects of criminology. Springfield, Ill.: Charles C. Thomas, 1968. 82 pages.

Hammer, Max. "Homosexuality in a women's reformatory." Corrective Psychiatry and Journal of Social Therapy, vol. 11, no. 3.

Hanson, Gary White. "Behavior modification of appointment attendance among youthful offenders." FCI Research Report (Tallahassee, Fla.), 3(2):20, 1971.

Harris, Thomas A. I'm OK—You're OK. New York: Harper & Row, 1967.

General Bibliography

Henderson, Richard L. "The correction officer and
    the educational program." American Journal
    of Correction (St. Paul, Minn.), 32(3):18-22,
    1970.

Hennepin County (Minn.) Court Services Department.
    Guided group interaction: theory and method,
    by Charles Larson. Minneapolis, 1970.
    71 pages. (Report 1)

Hindelang, Michael. "A learning theory analysis
    of the correctional process." Issues in
    Criminology (Berkeley, Calif.), 5(1):43-59,
    1970.

Hodge, Raymond. "The rehabilitation process: a
    prisoner's point of view." American Journal
    of Correction, 26(2):12-16, 1964.

Hogan, M. H. "Probation in Japan." Probation,
    17(1):8-11, 1971.

Hopper, C. B. "Conjugal visiting at the Missis-
    sippi State Penitentiary." Federal Proba-
    tion, vol. 28, 1964.

Huffman, Arthur V. "Problems precipitated by
    homosexual approaches." Journal of Social
    Therapy, vol. 7, 1961.

Huffman, Arthur V. "Sex deviation in a prison
    community." Journal of Social Therapy,
    vol. 6, 1960.

Hughes, H., et al. "Organizing the therapeutic
    potential of the addict prisoners community."
    International Journal of the Addictions, 2(2):
    205-223, 1970.

Hurlburt, Jack C., and Goss, John. "Developmental
    reading: an academic experiment for short-
    term institutions." American Journal of
    Correction, 29(6):18-21, 1967.

Hutchison, H. C. "Behavior theory, behavior
science, and treatment." Canadian Journal
of Corrections, 10(2):388-391, 1968.

Hutchison, H. C. "Learning theory, behavior
science, and treatment." Canadian Journal
of Corrections, 10(1):41-46, 1968.

Indiana Reformatory, Data Processing Center.
Comparative survey of 1,000 paroled immates'
educational history at the Indiana Reformatory. Pendleton, Ind., 1965. (mimeo)

Ingram, Gilbert L., and Minor, John A. "Shaping
the recreational behavior of psychopathic
delinquents." Journal of Correctional
Education (Menard, Ill.), 22(3):24-26, 1970.

Irwin, John. "Some research questions on homosexuality in jails and prisons." Revised
working paper for the conference on prison
homosexuality, October 14-15, 1971.

Irwin, Olive T. "Group therapy with juvenile
probationers." Federal Probation, 31(3):
57-63, 1967.

Jackson, Bruce. "Our prisons are criminal."
New York Times Magazine, Sept. 22, 1968,
pp. 45 ff.

Jacobson, Frank N., and McGee, Eugene N.
"Resistance to education." (Paper presented
at the Correctional Education Institute,
Federal Correctional Institution, El Reno,
Oklahoma, June 10-12, 1964.) Journal of
Correctional Education, 16(4):17-22, 1964.

Jeffrey, C. Ray, and Jeffrey, Ina A. "Delinquents
and dropouts: an experimental program in
behavior change." Canadian Journal of
Corrections, 12(1):47-58, 1970.

Jesness, Carl F., et al. "The search for effective treatment." Youth Authority Quarterly,
22(1):13-19, 1969.

199

General Bibliography

Jesness, Carl F., et al. The youth center research
    project. Sacramento, Calif.: American
    Justice Institute, 1972. (2 vols.)

John Howard Society of Saskatchewan. Vocational
    rehabilitation and corrections: proceedings
    of a seminar. Saskatoon, Canada, 1968.

Johnson, Elmer H. "Prerequisites to extension of
    prisoner education." Journal of Correctional
    Education, 17(4):17-19, 1965.

Johnson, Elmer H., and Britt, Benjamin. Self-
    mutilation in prisons: interaction of stress
    and social structure. Carbondale: Center
    for the Study of Crime, Delinquency, and
    Corrections, Southern Illinois University,
    1967.

Johnson, Lois M. "Transactional Analysis with
    juvenile delinquents." Transactional
    Analysis Bulletin, vol. III, no. 30.

Joint Commission on Correctional Manpower and
    Training. A model career ladder for proba-
    tion and parole agencies, by Rudy Sanfilippo
    and Jo Wallach. Washington, D.C., 1970.
    6 pages.

Jones, Howard. "Organization and group factors in
    approved school training," in The residential
    treatment of disturbed and delinquent boys,
    Cambridge (England) Institute of Criminology,
    1968, pp. 63-71.

Jones, Maxwell. Beyond the therapeutic community:
    social learning and social psychiatry. New
    Haven, Conn.: Yale University, 1968.
    150 pages.

Jones, Maxwell. Social Psychiatry in Practice.
    Baltimore, Md.: Penguin Books, 1968.

Jones, Maxwell. "Toward clarification of the
    therapeutic community." British Journal of
    Medical Psychology, 1960, 33.

Joselson, M. "Prison education: a major reason for its impotence." Corrective Psychiatry and Journal of Social Therapy (Prairie Village, Kansas), 17(2):48-56, 1972.

Karen, Robert L., and Bower, Roland C. "A behavioral analysis of a social control agency: Synanon." Journal of Research in Crime and Delinquency, 5(1):18-34, 1968.

Keefe, Thomas W., and Smith, Thomas H. "A group counseling and group counselor training program in an Air Force corrections setting." Corrective Psychiatry and Journal of Social Therapy, 16(1, 2, 3, & 4):97-102, 1970.

Kelly, T. W. "Vocational training in a correctional school: a new concept." International Child Welfare Review, 18(1-2):9-19, 1964.

Kentucky NewGate Project. Position paper submitted to NewGate Resource Center, NCCD Headquarters, Paramus, N.J. Ashland, Ky., 1972. 48 pages.

Kerkhofs, P., and Gilson, J. "Le group counselling en milieu penitentiaire." (Group counseling in the prison environment.) Bulletin de l'Administration Penitentiaire, 22(3):123-144, 1968.

Kimble, G. A. Hilgard and Maruis' Conditioning and Learning. New York: Appleton-Century-Crofts, 1961.

Kinney, Charles F. Parole authority perspectives: from penitentiary to university community—prospects and problems. 5 pages. No date. (mimeo)

Klapmuts, Nora. "Community alternatives to prison." Crime and Delinquency Literature, June, 1973.

General Bibliography

Korn, Richard R. "Issues and strategies of imple-
    mentation in the use of offenders in
    resocializing other offenders." Offenders as
    a correctional manpower source, Commission
    on Correctional Manpower and Training, 1968.

Kuhl, C. A. "Operant conditioning at Fricot."
    Youth Authority Quarterly, 22(1):20-23, 1969.

Kunzelmann, Harold P. "A strategy for experimen-
    tal teaching in an institutional setting."
    Journal of Correctional Education, 19(4):6-9,
    27-29, 1967.

Lantz, Helen, and Ingram, Gilbert. "The psycho-
    path and his response to behavior modifica-
    tion techniques." FCI Technical and Treatment
    Notes (Tallahassee, Fla.), 2(1):1-26, 1971.

Leiberg, Leon G. "'Project Challenge' begins
    operation at Lorton Youth Center." Journal
    of Correctional Education, 19(3):12-15, 1967.

Lenneer-Axelson, Barbro. "Group therapy among
    Swedish discharged recidivists." Howard
    Journal of Penology and Crime Prevention,
    12(4):297-299, 1969.

Lentchner, Lawrence H. "Group behavior therapy in
    a workshop setting." Corrective Psychiatry
    and Journal of Social Therapy, 14(2):84-95,
    1968.

Levine, R. V. "The MMPI and revised Beta as
    predictors of academic and vocational success
    in a correctional institution." FCI Research
    Report, 1(3):52, 1969. (Federal Correctional
    Institution, Tallahassee, Fla.)

Levinson, Robert B., Ingram, Gilbert L., and
    Azcarate, Eduardo. "'Aversive' group therapy:
    sometimes good medicine tastes bad." Crime
    and Delinquency, 14(4):336-339, 1968.

202

Lewis, Thomas M. "The role of the classroom teacher in a correctional institution." California Youth Authority Quarterly, 17(4): 20-22, 1964.

Libby, T. N. "The residential Centre for released prisoners." Canadian Journal of Corrections, 10(2):406-408, 1968.

Lievano, Jaime. "Group psychotherapy with adolescents in an industrial school for delinquent boys." Adolescence, 5(18):231-253, 1970.

London, Perry. "Behavior control," in U.S. National Commission on the Causes and Prevention of Violence, Task Force on Individual Acts of Violence, Crimes of Violence, vol. 13. Washington, D.C.: U.S. Government Printing Office, 1969, pp. 1359-1375.

Los Angeles County Probation Department. Reduction of delinquency through expansion of opportunity (RODEO). Los Angeles Probation Department, 1968. 40 pages.

MacCormick, Austin. Adult correctional institutions in the United States. Submitted to the President's Commission on Law Enforcement and Administration of Justice, Washington, D.C., 1967. 102 pages.

MacCormick, Austin. The education of adult prisoners, a survey and a program. New York: The National Society of Penal Information, 1931. 456 pages.

MacDonald, George J., Williams, Robinson, and Nichols, H. R. Treatment of the sex offender. Fort Steilacoom, Wash.: Western State Hospital, 1968. 23 pages.

Mackenzie, Louise L. "Service to inmates and staff." ALA Bulletin, 58(9):809-810, 1964.

General Bibliography

MacLennan, Beryce W., and Felsenfeld, Naomi. Group counseling and psychotherapy with adolescents. New York: Columbia University Press, 1968. 198 pages.

Macpherson, David P. "The role of new careerists." California Youth Authority Quarterly, 23(3): 31-35, 1970.

Maresh, Al. "Work training comes to the prison." American Journal of Correction, 31(4):30, 32, 1969.

Marohn, R. C. "The unit meeting: its implications for a therapeutic correctional community." International Journal of Group Psychotherapy, 17(2):159-167, 1967.

Marsh, John J., and Gares, Wayne. "NewGate: correctional education vs. education, psychology, and counseling." Educational Media (Spring):6-7, 19-22, 1972.

Massachusetts Correction Department. An evaluation of a mental health program in a maximum security correctional institution, by Frances J. Carney and Estelle D. Bottome. Boston, 1967. 18 pages. (Publication No. 803)

McCabe, M. Patrick, and Driscoll, Brian. College admission opportunities and the public offender. Presented to the American Association of College Admission Counselors (San Francisco), 1971. 27 pages.

McCaldon, R., et al. "Forensic seminar on reward and punishment." Canadian Journal of Corrections, 12(1):25-39, 1970.

McCollum, Sylvia G. "Say, have you got anything around here for a dummy?" Federal Probation (Washington, D.C.), 35(3):37-42, 1971.

McCormick, Paul. "Translation of delinquency language into TA." Transactional Analysis Bulletin, vol. IV, no. 16.

McCormick, Paul. "Why institutionalized offenders don't have to get better." _Transactional Analysis Bulletin_, vol. 4, no. 14.

McKee, John M. "The use of programmed instruction in correctional institutions." _Journal of Correctional Education_, 22(4):8-12, 28, 1970.

McPherson, Rupert. _Institutional vocational training and parole violation_. New York: New York University, 1961. 86 pages.

Michigan Corrections Department. _The use of correctional trade training_. Lansing, 1969. 47 pages.

Middle Atlantic State Conference of Correction. _Proceedings of the 32nd annual conference_, 1970, Baltimore, Md.

Miller, Eugene. "Education at Bucks County Prison." _American Journal of Correction_, 29(2):22-25, 1967.

Miller, Eugene, and Hughes, Rebecca. "New perspectives in the education of female prisoners." _Journal of Correctional Education_, 21(3):4-5, 20, 1969.

Miller, Michael J. "Future employment prospects and vocational training in prisons." _Georgia Journal of Corrections_ (Atlanta), 1(3):103-111, 1972.

Milnos, Agnes Eva. "The effects of a therapeutic community on the interpersonal relationships of a group of psychopaths." _British Journal of Criminology_, 9(1):22-38, 1969.

Minneapolis Rehabilitation Center. _The rehabilitation of parolees_, prepared by Richard C. Ericson and Daniel O. Moberg. Minneapolis, Minn., 1969. 134 pages.

General Bibliography

Minnesota Corrections Department. An analysis of
    the group residence for hard to place
    juvenile boys March 1971 to February 1972.
    Minnesota, 1972. 31 pages.

Minnesota Corrections Department, Research and
    Planning Division. Institution-community
    continuum: an analysis of population move-
    ment and program effectiveness, January 1,
    1970-December 31, 1970. St. Paul, 1971.
    20 pages.

Miron, Nathan B. "Behavior modification tech-
    niques in the treatment of self-injurious
    behavior in institutionalized retardees."
    Bulletin of Suicidology, No. 8. Washington,
    D.C.: U.S. Government Printing Office, 1971,
    pp. 64-69. (DHEW Publication No. [HSM] 71-
    9053)

Moore, Adrian L. Trabajo: a study of a voca-
    tional rehabilitation project for New
    Mexico's public offender population through
    the New Mexico Division of Vocational
    Rehabilitation, prepared for the New Mexico
    Council of the National Council on Crime and
    Delinquency. Albuquerque, 1968. 48 pages.

Moore, John E. "A.B.E.: a shot in the arm for
    correctional education programs." Journal of
    Correctional Education, 18(3):3, 30, 1966.

Morris, Delyte W. "The university's role in
    prison education." Nebraska Law Review,
    45(3):452-471, 1966.

Morris, Roger. "State programs in college educa-
    tion for inmates of correctional institu-
    tions." American Journal of Correction,
    30(2):20-22, 1968.

Morrison, J. W. "The effectiveness and benefit of
    correctional education: an evaluation of the
    Draper Correctional Program." Canadian
    Journal of Corrections, 10(2):428-431, 1968.

Morrison, June. "The use of volunteers in correctional education." Journal of Correctional
Education (Maryland), 23(1):20-26, 1971.

Mouk, Warren Stuart. "The effects of short-term
tasks and financial incentive on the
educational achievement of young prison
inmates." FCI Research Report, 1(7), 1969.
160 pages. (Federal Correctional Institution, Tallahassee, Fla.)

National Committee on Employment of Youth. Pros
and cons: new roles for nonprofessionals in
corrections, by Judith G. Benjamin, Marcia K.
Freedman, and Edith F. Lynton. New York,
1965. 133 pages.

National Council on Crime and Delinquency, Indiana
Citizens Council, Vocational Training Committee. Report. Indianapolis, 1966. 11 pages.

National Council on Crime and Delinquency, NewGate
Resource Center. NewGate directory: post-
secondary education programs in correctional
institutions. Paramus, N.J., 1972. 46
pages.

National Council on Crime and Delinquency. Report
of the (Professional Council) subcommittee on
study of the use of aides or assistants in
adult probation parole agencies. Paramus,
N.J., 1971. 51 pages.

National Institute of Labor Education, Mental
Health Program. The indigenous nonprofessional: a strategy of change in
community action and community health programs. New York, November 1964. 84 pages.
(mimeo)

National Institute of Mental Health. Behavior
modification in child and mental health—an
annotated bibliography on applications with
parents and teachers, by Daniel G. Brown.
Washington, D.C.: U.S. Government Printing
Office, 1971. 41 pages. (DHEW Publication
No. 71-9043)

General Bibliography

Neil, Thomas C.   "Education in the Alachua County
     jail." Journal of Correctional Education
     (Menard, Ill.), 22(4):15, 22, 1970.

New Jersey Vocational Education in Correctional
     Institutions Commission. Interim report.
     Trenton, N.J., 1971. 35 pages.

New York State Correction Department. Annual
     report of Division of Education, 1965.
     Albany, 1967. 43 pages.

New York State Correction Department. The New
     York State Vocational Institution: what it
     is and what it does. Albany, 1965. 22 pages.

New York University, Center for Social Policy and
     Program Development. Workshop on delinquency
     planning and the school to work transition.
     New York, 1970. 10 pages.

Nice, Richard W.   "The problems of homosexuality
     in corrections." American Journal of
     Correction, May-June, 1966.

Nice, Richard W.   "Treatment of the incarcerated
     drug user." American Journal of Correction,
     33(1):27-30, 1971.

Nichols, John D. A selected bibliography on
     training in correctional institutions with
     annotations developed for a partial list of
     this bibliography. Fayetteville: Arkansas
     Research Coordination Unit for Occupational
     Education, University of Arkansas, 1969.
     30 pages.

Nichols, John D. A study of Arkansas prison
     inmates concerning occupational training.
     Fayetteville: Arkansas Research Coordination
     Unit for Occupational Education, University
     of Arkansas, 1970. 27 pages.

Nichols, John D., and Brodsky, Stanley L.   "After
     they leave: a vocational follow-up study of
     former prisoners," in Brodsky, Stanley, and

Eggleston, Norman E., eds., The military prison. Carbondale: Southern Illinois University Press, 1970, pp. 159-160.

Nixon, R. A. Legislative dimensions of the new careers program: 1970. New York: New York University, Center for the Study of the Unemployed, 1970. 34 pages.

North Carolina Correction Department. 1970-71 educational services, by Robert W. Hyde and Shannon Roberts. Raleigh, N.C., 1971.

Ohio Mental Hygiene and Correction Department. "New Jobs for our convict craftsman." Motive, 11(2):18-23, 1965.

Oklahoma Vocational Rehabilitation Services. Vocational rehabilitation services in a state penitentiary system. Final report of a research and demonstration project Jan. 1, 1964 to June 30, 1967. 72 pages.

Ordway, John A. "Use of the offender's strengths in psychotherapy." Crime and Delinquency, 14(3):233-239, 1968.

Oregon State Board of Control, Corrections Division. An evaluation of the Upward Bound Oregon Prison Project. Salem, Ore.: State Board of Control, 1968. 20 pages.

Oregon State Board of Control, Research and Program Evaluation Division. A follow-up study of vocational programs at Oregon State Penitentiary and Oregon State Correctional Institution. Salem, Oregon, 1969. 58 pages.

O'Rourke, Thomas. "A descriptive study of suicide, attempted suicide and self-mutilation in New York City prisons." New York, unpublished, 1972.

Park, James W. "The unteachables." Journal of Correctional Education, 18(3):4-6, 31, 1966.

General Bibliography

Parlett, T. A. A., and Ayers, J. D. "The modifi-
    cation of criminal personality through massed
    learning by programed instruction." Canadian
    Journal of Criminology and Corrections
    (Ottawa), 13(2):155-165, 1971.

Pearl, Arthur, and Riessman, Frank. New careers
    for the poor. New York: Free Press, 1965.
    265 pages.

Pennsylvania, State Correctional Institution at
    Graterford. The paraprofessional law clinic:
    progress report, 1972. Graterford, Pa.,
    1972. 8 pages.

Peretti, Peter O. "Desocialization-resocializa-
    tion within the prison walls." Canadian
    Journal of Corrections, 12(1):59-66, 1970.

Peretti, Peter O. "Educational rehabilitation:
    prisoner attitude and inmate attendance."
    Prison Service Journal, 8(30):40-45, 1969.

Peters, Joseph J., et al. "Group psychotherapy
    of the sex offender." Federal Probation,
    32(3):41-45, 1968.

Peters, Joseph J., and Sadoff, Robert L.
    "Psychiatric services for sex offenders on
    probation." Federal Probation, 35(3):33-37,
    1971.

Phillips, Charles Elery, et al. The achievement
    place model: community based, family style,
    behavior modification programs for pre-
    delinquents. Santa Barbara, Calif.:
    Delinquency Prevention Strategy Conference,
    1970. 68 pages.

Pietsch, Karl. "Psychotherapy in a German
    prison." International Journal of Offender
    Therapy, 2(1):3-9, 1967.

Pilnick, Saul, et al. Collegefields: from delinquency to freedom. Report to the U.S. Health, Education, and Welfare Dept., Office of Juvenile Delinquency. Newark, N.J., 1967. 248 pages.

Pointer, Wesley Donald. Education and training versus maintenance and other prison work programs. Paper presented to Draper Conference on Manpower Development and Training in Correctional Programs. Montgomery, Alabama, 1967. 17 pages.

Pooley, Richard C. The control of human behavior in a correctional setting. Carbondale, Ill.: Center for the Study of Crime, Delinquency and Corrections, 1969. 27 pages.

Pownall, George A. Employment problems of released prisoners. University Park: University of Maryland, 1969. 319 pages.

President's Commission on Law Enforcement and Administration of Justice. Task Force Report: Corrections. U.S. Government Printing Office, 1967.

President's Commission on Law Enforcement and Administration of Justice. The Challenges of Crime in a Free Society. U.S. Government Printing Office, 1967.

Price, Joseph. "Guided group interaction: a peer group approach." Youth Authority Quarterly, 22(2):22-35, 1969.

Progress for Providence. Laying it on the line . . . a report on the Providence Youth Interviews Project. Providence, R.I., 1966. 112 pages.

Rapkin, Robert M. "The NARA unit at Danbury: a short history of a unique treatment program for heroin addicts." American Journal of Correction, 33(2):24-26, 1971.

General Bibliography

Rappaport, Richard G. "Group therapy in prison."
    International Journal of Group Psychotherapy,
    21(4):489-496, 1971.

Ray, Edward T., and Kilburn, Kent L. "Behavior
    modification techniques applied to community
    behavior problems." Criminology (Beverly
    Hills, Calif.), 8(2):173-184, 1970.

Rehabilitation Research Foundation, Draper
    Correctional Center. An ecological experi-
    ment in corrections: a programed environment
    for behavior modification. Elmore, Ala.,
    1971. 20 pages.

Rehabilitation Research Foundation, Draper
    Correctional Center. Experimental manpower
    laboratory for corrections: second progress
    report, December 1, 1968-January 31, 1969.
    Elmore, Ala., 1969. 56 pages.

Resnik, H. L. P., and Peters, J. J. "Outpatient
    group therapy with convicted pedophiles."
    International Journal of Group Psychotherapy,
    17(2):151-158, 1967.

Richmond, Mark S. Prison profiles. Dobbs Ferry,
    N.Y.: Oceana, 1965. 203 pages.

Rieger, Wolfram. "Suicide attempts in a federal
    prison." Archives of General Psychiatry,
    June, 1971, vol. 24.

Riessman, Frank, and Popper, Hermine I., eds.
    Up from Poverty: New Career Ladders for
    Nonprofessionals. New York: Harper & Row,
    1968.

Rinsley, Donald B. "The adolescent in residential
    treatment: some critical reflections."
    Adolescence, 2(5):83-95, 1967.

Ritter, Joseph. "Youth rehabilitation programme."
    Community Schools Gazette (Southport, Eng.),
    66(2):61-66, 1972.

Roberts, Albert R. "Current trends in college-
level instruction for inmates of correctional institutions." Journal of Correctional Education, 21(4):34-47, 1969.

Roberts, Albert R. "Developmental perspective
of correctional education." American
Journal of Correction, 31(3):14-17, 1969.

Roberts, Albert R. Sourcebook on prison education: past, present, and future.
Springfield, Ill.: Charles C. Thomas, 1971.

Roberts, Albert R. "Vocational highlights of
three correctional education programs."
Journal of Correctional Education, 22(1):
34-38, 1970.

Robison, James. The California Prison, Parole
and Probation System, California Assembly
Office of Research, 1969.

Robison, James, and Smith, Gerald. "The effectiveness of correctional programs." Crime
and Delinquency, 17(1), 1971.

Robitscher, Jonas B. "Non-coercive therapy in
a prison setting." Prison Journal, 48(2):
38-42, 1968.

Romano, Mary Elizabeth. "Helping 'pre-offenders'
in school." International Journal of
Offender Therapy, 14(1):36-40, 1970.

Rosenstein, Sherwin H., and Hersen, Michel.
"Resistances encountered in outpatient group
psychotherapy with male juvenile probationers." Corrective Psychiatry and Journal of
Social Therapy, 15(2):45-49, 1969.

Rosow, Jerome M. "The role of jobs in a new
national strategy against crime." Federal
Probation (Washington, D.C.), 35(2):14-18,
1971.

Roth, Loren H.   "Territoriality and homosexuality
    in a male prison population." American
    Journal of Orthopsychiatry (New York),
    41(3):510-513, 1971.

Rubin, Julius. "Crime and punishment." Correc-
    tive Psychiatry and Journal of Social
    Therapy, 13(3):162-170, 1967.

Ryan, T. A. Adult basic education in corrections
    program: overview. Honolulu, Education
    Research and Development Center, 1972.
    9 pages.

Schmidberg, Melitta. "Reality therapy with
    offenders: principles." International
    Journal of Offender Therapy, 14(1):19-26,
    1970.

Schwitzgebel, Ralph. Development and legal
    regulation of coercive behavior modification
    techniques with offenders. Chevy Chase,
    Md.: Center for Studies of Crime and Delin-
    quency, 1971. (Crime and Delinquency
    Issues: Public Health Service Publication
    No. 2067)

Schwitzgebel, Ralph. "Short-term operant condi-
    tioning of adolescent offenders on socially
    relevant variables." Journal of Abnormal
    Psychology, 72(2):134-142, 1967.

Schwitzgebel, Ralph, and Kolb, D. A. "Inducing
    behavior changes in adolescent delinquents."
    Behavioral Research and Therapy, (1):297-
    304, 1964.

Scura, William C., and Eisenman, Russell.
    "Punishment learning in psychopaths with
    social and non-social reinforcers."
    Corrective Psychiatry and Journal of Social
    Therapy (Kansas), 17(1):58-64.

Seay, Donna M. "The roles of the teacher for the
    effective use of P.I. in a correctional
    setting." Journal of Correctional Education,
    20(1):12-18, 26, 1968.

Sessions, Arnold. A report on jail educational programs of selected cities and counties in the United States. Co-sponsored by the Seattle Community College and the King County Sheriffs Dept. 18 pages.

Shah, Saleem A. "Some basic principles and concepts of behavior modification," in Conference on the social restoration of offenders through manpower development and training, November 1967. New York: Wakoff Research Center, 1967. 18 pages.

Shapiro, Michael H. "The uses of behavior control technologies: a response." Issues in Criminology (Berkeley, Calif.), 7(2):55-93, 1972.

Shobald, Richard H. Doing my own time. Garden City, N.Y.: Doubleday & Co., 1972. 270 pages.

Sluga, W. "Psychodrama in a psychiatric prison." Howard Journal of Penology and Crime Prevention, 13(1):30-34, 1970.

Southern Illinois University, Center for the Study of Crime, Delinquency and Corrections. Development laboratory for correctional training: Final report. Carbondale, Ill. 134 pages. (mimeo)

Spece, Roy G. "Conditioning and other technologies used to 'treat?' 'rehabilitate?' 'demolish?' prisoners and mental patients." Southern California Law Review (Los Angeles), 46(2):616-684, 1972.

Stagner, Harold W. "Delinquents, through motivation, are taught to read." Journal of Correctional Education, 20(1):23-24, 1968.

Stephenson, Richard M., and Scarpetti, Frank R. "Essexfields: a non-residential experiment in group centered rehabilitation of delinquents." American Journal of Correction, 31(1):12-18, 1969.

Sturup, G. K. Treating the "untreatable":
    chronic criminals at Herstedvester.
    Baltimore: Johns Hopkins Press, 1968.
    206 pages.

Sullivan, John C., and Bobo, Marvin O. Syllabus
    for adult education tutoring program in a
    penal institution. Marion, Ill.: U.S.
    Penitentiary, 1970. 160 pages.

Sunner, S. H. "Vocational guidance for delin-
    quent girls." Approved Schools Gazette,
    62(3):129-131, 1968.

Switzer, Mary E. "Vocational rehabilitation and
    corrections: a promising partnership."
    Federal Probation, 31(3):12-17, 1967.

Sykes, Gresham. "Prison riots: struggle for
    power." Nation, May 7, 1959.

Sykes, Gresham. The Society of Captives.
    Princeton, N.J.: Princeton University
    Press, 1958.

Taggart, Robert. The prison of unemployment:
    manpower programs for offenders. Baltimore:
    Johns Hopkins University Press, 1972.
    116 pages.

Tait, Downing C. "A 'therapeutic community' for
    selected families." Mental Hygiene, 52(1):
    45-49, 1968.

Taylor, A. J. W. "An evaluation of group psycho-
    therapy in a girls' borstal." International
    Journal of Group Psychotherapy, 17(2):168-
    177, 1967.

Terwilliger, Carl. "The nonprofessional in
    correction." Crime and Delinquency, 12(3):
    227-285, 1966.

Texas Corrections Department. Recidivism among
    general education development program
    graduates, by Richard C. Jones. Austin,
    1969.

216

Thomas, Herbert E. "Regressive maladaptive behavior in maximum security prisoners." Revised working paper for the conference on prison homosexuality, Oct. 14-15, 1971.

Thompson, G. R. "Institutional programs for female offenders." Canadian Journal of Corrections, 10(2):438-441, 1968.

Thorne, G. L., Tharpe, R. G., and Wetzel, R. L. "Behavior modification techniques: new tools for probation officers." Federal Probation, (31):21-27, 1967.

Toch, Hans. Violent Men. Chicago: Aldine, 1969.

Tomkins, Calvin. "Crime breeding prisons." Newsweek, April 25, 1960.

Torrence, J. T. "Prison vocational data processing." Journal of Correctional Education, 17(3):16-18, 1965.

Torrence, J. T. "Space age programs in correctional institutions." Journal of Correctional Education, 17(1):17-19, 1965.

U.S. Education Office, Educational Personnel Development Bureau. Project development proposal for improvement of staff in institutions for delinquent children: final report, by Andrew W. Halpin, James B. Kenney, and Andrew E. Hayes. Athens: University of Georgia Press, 1969. 48 pages.

U.S. Education Office. Opening doors through educational programs for institutionalized delinquents. Washington, D.C.: U.S. Government Printing Office, 1967. 40 pages.

U.S. Manpower Policy, Evaluation and Research Office. Training needs in correctional institutions. Washington, D.C., 1966. 21 pages.

General Bibliography

U.S. National Clearinghouse for Mental Health
Information. Research in individual psychotherapy: a bibliography. Chevy Chase, Md.,
1969. 167 pages.

U.S. President's Committee on Juvenile Delinquency
and Youth Crime. Training for new careers:
the community apprentice program. Washington,
D.C., June 1965. 107 pages.

U.S. Prisons Bureau. Board of Directors' annual
report—1967. Washington, D.C.: Federal
Prison Industries, 1967. 21 pages.

U.S. Prisons Bureau. Correctional education: a
bibliography. Washington, D.C., 1972.
13 pages.

University of Cambridge, Institute of Criminology.
The education of offenders, compiled by D. L.
Howard. Cambridge, Eng., 1972. 31 pages.
(Bibliographical Series No. 5)

University of Chicago, Center for Studies in
Criminal Justice. Second progress report
(July 1, 1969-June 1, 1970) of the probation
officer-case aide project, by Donald W.
Beless and William S. Pilcher. Chicago,
1970.

University of Hawaii, Juvenile Delinquency and
Youth Development Center. Application of
behavior modification techniques of Hawaii.
Honolulu, 1968. 29 pages.

University of Southern California, Youth Studies
Center. The role of the institutional
teacher, a report on a pilot training program, by Gilbert Geis, Houshang Poorkaj, and
Ronald Honnard. Los Angeles, 1964. 134
pages. (Youth Studies Center Training
Report No. 1)

Vedder, Clyde, and King, Patricia. Problems of
Homosexuality in Corrections. Springfield,
Ill.: Charles C. Thomas, 1971.

Wakoff Research Center. Restoration of Youth
    Through Training: a final report, by
    Clyde E. Suhlivan and Wallace Mandell.
    Staten Island, N.Y., 1967. 393 pages.

Waldo, Gordon P. "Research in correctional
    education." Journal of Correctional Educa-
    tion, 21(4):4-9, 1969.

Warren, M. Q. "The case for differential treat-
    ment of delinquents." The Annals of the
    American Academy of Political and Social
    Science, 381, January 1969.

Washburn, Richard W. "Experimental learning for
    confined delinquents." Human Relations
    Training News, 14(1):3-5, 1970.

Washington (State), Vocational Rehabilitation
    Division. Seattle project of the Federal
    Offenders Rehabilitation Program (RD 2079-g),
    November, 1965-February, 1969. Olympia,
    Wash., 1969. 76 pages.

Washington Western State Hospital. Annual Report:
    July 1, 1970-June 30, 1971. Treatment pro-
    gram for the sexual offender. Fort
    Steilacoom, Wash., 1972. 4 pages.

Waters, P. D. "Technology brings new learning
    environments." Community Schools Gazette
    (London), 64(6):331-334, 1970.

Weber, J. Robert. "A report of the juvenile
    institutions project." Unpublished report
    to the Osborne Association at the NCCD,
    September 1966.

Weir, J. D. "Academic and vocational programs in
    Canadian Penitentiary Service." Journal of
    Correctional Education, 19(2):18-19, 1967.

Wetzel, Ralph. "Use of behavioral techniques in a
    case of compulsive stealing." Journal of
    Consulting Psychology, 30(5):367-374, 1966.

Whitely, J. Stuart. "The response of psycho-
    paths to a therapeutic community." British
    Journal of Psychiatry, 115(534):517-529,
    1970.

Whitely, J. Stuart. "The treatment of delin-
    quents in a therapeutic community." Howard
    Journal of Penology and Crime Prevention,
    12(3):183-190, 1968.

Wickman, James R. "Counseling-teaching the
    youthful offender." Journal of Correctional
    Education, 20(1):21-22, 1968.

Wilkerson, Wallace W. "Psychiatric consultation
    with probationers and parolees." Federal
    Probation, 33(2):45-50, 1969.

Willetts, David A. "The college behind bars."
    Welfare Reporter, 22(3):19-21, 1971.

Wilson, John M., and Snodgrass, Jon D. "The
    prison code in a therapeutic community."
    Journal of Criminal Law, Criminology and
    Police Science, 60(4):472-478, 1969.

Wisconsin, Department of Health and Social
    Services, Bureau of Research. Camp Flambeau
    project. (Statistical Bulletin 664.)
    Madison: Dept. of Health and Social
    Services, 1968. 20 pages.

Wold, Robert. "An experiment in academic struc-
    ture." Educational Media, 3(6):8, 11, 1971.

Wright, W. F. "Treatment program at the Recep-
    tion, Diagnostic and Treatment Centre,
    Grandview School, Galt, Ontario." Canadian
    Journal of Corrections, 10(2):337-345, 1968.

Yalom, Irvin D. "Group therapy of incarcerated
    sexual deviants," in Gochros, H., and
    Schultz, LeRoy, eds., Human sexuality and
    social work. New York: Association Press,
    1972, pp. 186-204.

Yanagimoto, Masharu. "Some features of the Japanese prison system." British Journal of Criminology (London), 10(3):209-224, 1970.

Zimberoff, Steven J. "Behavior and modification with delinquents." Correctional Psychologist, 3(6):11-25, 1968.

INDEX

223

Index

224

Index

Education (cont.)
  psychology, 168
  staff, 124-127
  status, 3
Educational rehabilitation,
    136-147
Effectiveness, treatment,
    165-167
Effeminacy, 114
Ego states, 24-25, 27-28
Emotions, 3, 23, 25
  control, 40
  unstable, 102
Employment: See Work
Environment, 51
  early, 42
  vs. heredity, 58
  home, 68
  institutional, 50, 61, 64,
    66, 67, 95
  mastery, 25
  prison, 99, 101, 105, 107,
    111-112, 149
  single-sex, 115, 116
  social, 33, 34, 50
  street, 22, 50
Environmental stimuli, 56
Equivalency test, high
    school, 137-138
ERNST, F., 29
Escape, 60, 94, 120
Essexfields (N.J.), 152-153
Ethnic groups, 97
Evaluation methods, 1, 6,
    1-10
Ex-offenders: on-staff, 87
  as manpower, 80-81
  as students, 146
Expectations, 68, 104
Exploiters, 93
EYSENCK, H. J., 56

Facilities, limited, 91-92
Families, pseudo-, 113
Family environments, 43, 52
Family live-ins, 119-120
Family problems, 5

Family stability, 102
Family therapy, 161
Family ties, 120, 121, 155
Female offenders, 115
  dance programs, 131
  homosexual, 109, 112, 113
FERRI, E., 60
Financial incentives, 65
  See also Token economy
Financial factors, 2, 86, 90,
    91, 133, 150
  See also Economic factors
Fines, 63
First-time offenders, 2
Florida Division of Youth
    Services, 52
Florida State University, 168
Fondling, 26
Forgers, 6
Forgiveness, 176
Foster homes, 151, 155, 176
FOX, V., 116
FREEDMAN, M. K., 84
Freedom, 112
FREUD, S., 14
Frequency, violation, 132
Friendship, 52
Frustration, 25, 99, 122, 129

Game state, 23
Games, 27-29, 50
Games People Play (Berne), 23
Genetic abnormalities, 58
"Ghettoized" jobs, 86
GLASSER, W., 14, 22, 171-177
GLENN, J., 138
GOFFMAN, E., 95
Goree Unit of Texas Department
    of Corrections, 131
"Grapevines," 112
"Gripe sessions," 48
GRODER, M., 28, 29
Group counseling, 152, 161
Group dynamics, 34
Group homes, 155-159, 176
Group leaders, 47-48, 50, 53,
    79-80
Group meetings, 126-127, 156

226

Index

Instrumental conditioning:
See Operant conditioning
Integration, personality, 7
Intelligence, 140
Interaction: social, 23, 40
See also Guided Group
Interaction (GGI); Inmate/
staff relations; Patient/
staff relations; Thera-
peutic community (TC)
Internships, 168
Interpersonal Maturity Class-
ification System, 7-8
Interpersonal relations, 18,
129, 130
See also Group therapy;
Inmate/staff relations;
Patient/staff relations;
Social relations; Thera-
peutic community (TC)
Intervention, community,
68-70
See also Community-based
corrections
Interviewing, 9, 10, 56, 102
Irish Progressive Stage Sys-
tems of Correction, 62
Irresponsibility, 20, 35,
172, 174
See also Antisocial behav-
ior; Asocial behavior
Isolation, 64, 99, 101,
116-117, 150

Jail-building moratorium,
163-164
Jails, 137-138
Job placement, 136, 146
See also Work
Job training: See Vocational
rehabilitation
JOHNSON, E., 102
JONES, M., 34-35, 39
Judicial inequities, 95, 96
Judicial lenience, 101
Juvenile delinquents: See
Delinquents
Juvenile recidivists, 114

KARPMAN, B., 111
KERLE, K. E., 143
Kidnaping, 94
KILBURN, K., 66
KIUD, 28
KLAPMUTS, N., 149

Labeling, 11
See also Classification
Labor unions, 92, 136
Ladders (lines), career, 78-79,
84-86
LAIRD, C. A., 142, 143
Language, transactional
analysis, 23
Language barriers, 95, 104
Language competence, 140, 141
LANTZ, H., 71
Lateness, 85
Latin Americans, 102
Laughing, uncontrollable, 131
Law Enforcement Assistance
Administration, 137
Leaders, group, 47-48, 50, 53,
79-80
Leadership, 40, 44, 94
Learning, 17, 39-40, 58, 134-135
See also Conditioning; Educa-
tion; Living-learning
situations; Training
Legal action, 116, 119
Legal status, prisoners', 3
Legislators, 90
Lenience, judicial, 101
Lesbianism, 109, 112, 113
Levels of Interpersonal
Maturity, 7
Libraries, 138-140
Life positions, 26-27
Literacy, 138, 140
Live-ins, family, 119-120
Living accommodations, 62
See also Housing
Living-learning situations, 39-41
Long Island University, 168
LOUGHERY, D. L., 81, 82
Lying, 66
LYNTON, E. F., 84

228

Index

Index

Index